CW00706851

THE JUICE 2009

The Juice 2009
by Matt Skinner

The Juice Team and Mitchell Beazley would like to send a big thank you to all the wine merchants, agents, retailers, and producers who helped with the research for this edition of the book.

First published in Great Britain in 2008 by Mitchell Beazley, an imprint of Octopus Publishing Group Ltd, 2–4 Heron Quays, London E14 4JP. www.octopusbooks.co.uk

An Hachette Livre UK Company www.hachettelivre.co.uk

ISBN 978 1 84533 391 1

A CIP catalogue record for this book is available from the British Library.

Set in Helvetica

Colour reproduction by AltaImages in the UK
Printed and bound by R R Donnelley in China

Commissioning Editor: Rebecca Spry
Managing Editor: Hilary Lumsden
Project Editor: Leanne Bryan
Copy-editor: Samantha Stokes
Proofreader: Susan Keevil
Deputy Art Director: Yasia Williams-Leedham
Concept Design: Matt Utber
Layout Design: Eoghan O'Brien
Photographer: Chris Terry
Production Manager: Peter Hunt

Contents

Welcome

With the health of our planet in pretty dire shape, and the wine industry braced to feel the effects of climate change long before most, I thought that this year would be as good a time as any to look at the efforts and initiatives of those producers working against the odds to make a difference. Producers who are working to make packaging lighter, to build and develop energy efficient wineries, to conserve water, and to grow and produce in the most natural way possible. Producers who are trying to leave things in a better shape than they found them in. Producers who I believe are worthy of your support.

The more research I did for this year's edition, the more I got thinking about what we do to produce the book, and how we might do it more efficiently. For starters, we cut out all of the travel that was undertaken to produce the photography for previous editions. Instead we just gathered up our gear and walked around the block to Holborn Studios, where we laid out a giant collage of every photograph we'd ever taken. We then put up a huge ladder and made Chris Terry climb to the top and take even more lovely photos of, well, all of his lovely photos. It was a beautiful thing and these pictures form the basis for the images you'll find over the coming pages.

I also learned that there are plenty more things I could be doing to make this process a little kinder on Mother Nature. Don't get me wrong: just because I've made a few small changes, by no means do I think I'm perfect, but it's a start, and like many of the producers I've included in this year's guide, I'm committed to making more changes as we go forward.

Matt

How It All Works

What began life as a weekly email sent out to friends and workmates in a vain attempt to help them drink better, has now become a regular distillation of my drinking year. As with previous editions, The Juice 2009 combines 100 wine recommendations together with a few handy tips and a little bit of wisdom. Think of it as the big kids' survival guide to Planet Wine, or better still, a huge step toward better drinking.

So here's the drill. I thought that rather than ranking the wines 1 to 100, it'd be far more useful if I grouped the wines by occasion, and so as with previous years I've split our 100 wines into five easy groups of 20 wines each: DRINK, GIVE, DINE, SPLURGE, and STASH. There's something here for everyone: every taste, every budget, and every occasion.

As per last year, I've made every effort to ensure that both price and vintage (the current release has been reviewed wherever possible) are as accurate as possible at the time of publication. Listed stockists are a mixture of supermarkets, national chains, smaller independent wine retailers, and online merchants – the idea being that you should be able to get your hands on most of the following 100 wines without too much heartache.

Happy drinking!

The Juice Awards

Awards time always brings about a certain sense of dread. For starters, there is very deliberately no ranking system in *The Juice*: there are no star ratings and no scores out of 100. Pedestals are not what this guide has ever been about. Irrespective of price, each of the wines featured in this book deserves to be here for one reason or another. That said, throughout the course of the year, there are always one or two wines and one or two names that repeatedly crop up, and so for that reason I think it's important you know who and what these stellar achievers are. So, without apology, these are the wines that I talked about, enthused about, and repeatedly sniffed, swirled, and slurped this year.

WINE OF THE YEAR

Isole e Olena Cepparello 2003
Tuscany, Italy

Paulo de Marchi's meticulous approach and incredible attention to detail have seen his estate's flagship wine, Cepparello, grow to develop a much-deserved, near cult-like international following. Dreamed up by de Marchi in the late 1970s, Cepparello is assembled from the very best parcels of estate-grown Sangiovese from vineyards perched around 400 metres above sea level. The resulting wines are characterized by incredible depth and purity, and an uncanny ability to age. From the vintage produced during the blisteringly-hot summer of 2003, this example illustrates how, even in the toughest of years, great producers will still make great wines. The end result is spellbinding. Walk over hot coals, sell vital organs, do whatever it takes to get your hands on this incredible wine.

BARGAIN OF THE YEAR

De Bortoli Gulf Station
Pinot Noir 2007
Yarra Valley, Australia

This is ridiculously cheap and yet phenomenally good Pinot Noir. De Bortoli has really raised the bar with this cracking example that effortlessly ticks all of the right boxes. For starters you get terrific varietal character: sweet cherry, smoke, and spice coupled with silky mouth-feel and bright acidity. There's even a small lick of attractive French oak in there just to really add insult to injury. It's all there, and largely thanks to the men behind the controls, Steve Webber and Bill Downie. A cracking wine that just goes from strength to strength.

PRODUCER OF THE YEAR

De Bortoli Wines
Australia

De Bortoli are on quite a roll at the moment. With much recent attention given to their Yarra Valley operation, it would seem that the quality of pretty much everything in the company portfolio – that includes 25 different brands sourced from a similar number of varieties and regions – has also risen in the process. And that's no mean feat. In all, three De Bortoli wines grace the pages of this year's guide, their Gulf Station Pinot Noir 2007 taking the award for Bargain of the Year. And, while much has changed (and grown) since De Bortoli's inception in 1928, the best thing about this family-owned operation is that it has never lost sight of its market, nor forgotten that great wine is made in the vineyard.

Varieties, Places, and Styles

Wine comes in all different shapes and sizes; big wines, little wines, fat wines, skinny wines, good wines, great wines, and wines that will absolutely blow your mind. And while what happens in the winery can play a big role in determining how a wine might end up tasting, grape variety, place, and style will all have an impact too. With the number of varieties and styles now running well into the four figures, here's a brief run-down of those that grace the pages of this year's edition of *The Juice*.

THE WHITES

Chablis (*SHA-blee*)

Chablis is the name of a town in the northern-most part of Burgundy in France. The area's ancient Kimmeridgian limestone soils are unique and produce fine, pristine, mineral-like white wines, made out of Burgundy's white star, Chardonnay. With the use of new oak largely frowned upon in Chablis, the best examples display soft stone/citrus fruit, honey, river-rock, hay, mineral, and cashew character. Trademark mouthwatering acidity ensures the best examples are with us for years.

Chardonnay (*SHAR-do-nay*)

Love it or loathe it, you can't deny this grape its place in wine's hall of fame. Some of the very best examples hail from Burgundy, where texture, finesse, structure, and ageing ability rule over simple "drink-now" fruit flavours. You see, Chardonnay comes in all different shapes and sizes. Flavours range from the delicate, citrus, and slightly honeyed styles of Chablis to warmer, Southern-hemisphere styles, where aromas range from peaches and pears to full-throttle, ripe, tropical fruits like banana, pineapple, guava, and mango.

Chenin Blanc (*shuh-NIN BLAHN*)

Handier than a Swiss army knife, the globetrotting Chenin's high natural acidity and tendency to flirt with botrytis lend it equally well to a variety of styles: sweet, dry, or fizzy. A good traveller, Chenin's stomping ground is France's Loire Valley, where it makes racy dry whites, luscious sweet wines, and clean, frothy fizz. Expect aromas of apples, gooseberries, and fresh herbs.

Gewurztraminer
(geh-VERZ-trah-MEE-ner)
Like a drag queen with too much make-up and perfume (and little shame), this is the incredibly camp member of the white-grape family. In reality, Gewurz is one of the superstar varieties of Alsace in France. The best ooze aromas of lychee, rose, orange blossom, cinnamon, ginger, and spice. Good Gewurz will be rich and weighty, with great length of flavour.

Marsanne *(mar-SAHN)*
Clean, fresh, and fruity, this grape plays second fiddle to Viognier in France's northern Rhône Valley; however, it dominates many of the white-wine blends of the southern Rhône.

Expect ripe, peachy fruit flavours, fresh acidity, and barely a whiff of oak. With a bit of age, Marsanne takes on an amazing honeyed character and becomes slightly oilier, with more weight and richness. Outside France, you might see it in parts of Australia.

Muscat
For purposes of this book, the large Muscat family of grapes can be split into non-identical triplets: Muscat Blanc à Petits Grains, Muscat of Alexandria, and Muscat Ottonel. Wine styles vary from light, fizzy Moscato d'Asti (northwest Italy) and sweet, spirity Muscat de Beaumes-de-Venise (France's Rhône Valley) to Spain's aromatic Málagas and the unique liqueur Muscats of Australia's northeast Victoria.

Palomino Fino
(pal-o-MEEN-o FEEN-o)
The most important variety in the production of sherry, accounting for four of the five main styles: manzanilla,

fino, amontillado, and oloroso. Fino is the most popular and one of the greatest food wines in the world. The best are bone-dry, nutty, and slightly salty, with great mineral texture and a clean, tangy finish.

Pedro Ximénez (*PAY-dro hee-MAY-neth*)

Although "PX", as it's more commonly called, falls into the white-grape family, this sun-loving variety produces sweet, thick, syrupy wines. Great examples are almost black in colour, viscous, and super-sweet, with intense aromas of raisin and spice.

Pinot Gris/Pinot Grigio (*PEE-no gree/PEE-no GREE-jee-o*)

Technically, these are the same grape; the key difference lies in the style. Pinot Grigio tends to be light, delicate, and fresh, usually made in stainless-steel tanks and best drunk young, when it's zippy and vibrant. Pinot Gris is fatter and richer, with more weight and intensity, often from time spent in oak. Pinot Grigio is commonly found in the cool of northeast Italy, while Pinot Gris is never more at home than in the French region of Alsace.

Riesling (*REES-ling*)

Technically brilliant, but still a wee bit nerdy, Riesling currently represents some of this planet's great bargain wine buys. While its spiritual home is Germany, you'll find world class examples from Austria, France, and Australia. The best will have beautiful, pure, citrus fruit aromas alongside fresh-cut flowers and spice, with flavours of lemons, limes, and minerals.

Sauvignon Blanc (*SO-vin-yon BLAHN*)

Think passion-fruit, gooseberry, elderflower, blackcurrant… even cat's pee! France, South Africa, Chile, and Australia all have a good crack at it, but New Zealand (Marlborough, to be exact) is the modern home of this variety. The best examples are pale, unmistakably pungent on the nose, painfully crisp, and ultra-refreshing with plenty of zip and racy acidity.

Sémillon (*SEM-ee-yon*)

Sémillon is native to Bordeaux in France, but it's down under in New South Wales's Hunter Valley that Semillon (note the lack of accent on the "e") has had greatest success, producing beautifully crafted and insanely long-lived wines. In its youth, great examples explode with pear, white peach, and other ripe summer fruits. But stash a bottle away for a rainy day a few years down the line, and you'll witness this variety's true magic: aromas of super-intense citrus fruit – even marmalade – alongside toast, honey, nuts, and sweet spice.

Sherry

Sherry is the English term for the wine-producing region of Jerez-de-la-Fontera in Spain's Andalucia. There are a number of styles produced in the sherry-producing triangle down there, from a number of different varieties. Wine styles can run anywhere from bone-dry to super-sweet, while the key grape varieties used to produce them are Palomino Fino, Pedro Ximénez, and Moscatel.

Verdicchio (*vehr-DIK-ee-o*)

Verdicchio is grown and produced in Italy's Marche region, making big, rich whites that are pretty neutral when it comes to aroma, but super-lemony in flavour with plenty of spice and richness. Because of its weight, it can handle oak, too, so expect to see some wooded examples.

Viognier (*vee-ON-yay*)

Viognier overflows with intoxicating aromas of apricots, orange rind, and fresh-cut flowers. It's weighty, rich, and oily in texture, with great length and beautifully soft acidity. Native to France's northern Rhône, it also shows promise in Australia and South Africa.

THE REDS

Cabernet Sauvignon
(KAB-er-nay SO-veen-yon)
King of the red grapes; the best display power, finesse, elegance, the ability to age, and universal appeal. Its home was Bordeaux, but particularly good examples now also come from Italy, Spain, Chile, Argentina, South Africa, Australia, and California. The range of flavours and aromas varies greatly, but look for blackcurrant, dark cherry, and plummy fruit alongside cedar, mint, and eucalyptus.

Carmenère _(car-meh-NAIR)_
Carmenère can be a nightmare in the vineyard: it's hard to get ripe, and once it is, you have a tiny window in which to pick it before the acidity disappears. But when it's good, it's really good! Bearing an uncanny likeness to Merlot, the best examples are bursting with super-dark fruits (plums, blackberries, and black cherries) and aromas of spice and leather.

Chianti _(ki-AN-tee)_
Chianti is a region in Tuscany made up of eight distinct subdistricts, including Colli Senesi, Classico, and Rufina. It circles the city of Florence and extends toward Sienna in the South. There are eight grape varieties permitted for use in Chianti, although few producers nowadays use all eight (some of which are white), with many preferring to focus on Tuscany's native red star, Sangiovese. Increasingly, Merlot, Cabernet Sauvignon, and Syrah are being used to "bulk up" Sangiovese's often lean and skeletal frame.

Grenache _(GRIN-ash)_
Grown widely in Spain, France, and Australia, Grenache is the workhorse of red grapes, and can be a stand-alone performer in its own right. As concentrated, weighty, fully-fledged reds (especially in France's southern Rhône), the wines sit comfortably alongside some of the world's greatest. Grenache also provides the base for many rosés:

its low tannin, acidity, and good whack of alcohol go perfect in pink.

Malbec
This red grape variety loves the sun and is found in Argentina's Andes Mountains (home to a handful of the highest-altitude vineyards on earth). These are big wines, and the best are soft and super-fruity, with plums and spice.

Merlot (*MER-low*)
Merlot has long played second fiddle to Big Brother Cabernet, often sidelined for blending. Yet it's the most widely planted red grape in Bordeaux, and in recent times, both California and Australia have developed a love affair with it. New World examples tend to be plump, with ripe, plummy fruit and naturally low tannin. Wines from north of the equator are drier, leaner, and generally less in-your-face.

Mourvèdre (*moor-VED-rah*)
The star of the southern Rhône. Along with dark, sweet fruit there's mushroom, tobacco, roast lamb – even the elephant pen at the zoo! In Spain, it's known as Monastrell and Mataro, while in Australia it goes by Mataro and Mourvèdre. Because of its funkiness, it's rarely produced as a solo variety and is usually reserved for blending.

Nebbiolo (*neb-ee-YO-lo*)
The best examples of Nebbiolo are layered and complex, oozing aromas of tar, roses, dark cherry, black olives, and rosemary. In great wines, concentrated fruit, firm acidity, and a wash of drying tannins ensure that they'll go the distance if you want to stash them away. Nebbiolo's home is Piedmont, where it stacks up to everything, from mushrooms (truffles) to chicken, rabbit, and all sorts of game right through to good old, mouldy cheeses.

Pinot Noir (*PEE-no NWAR*)
Top examples of Pinot are seductive, intriguing, even sexy, and their versatility with food is near unrivalled.

Thought of as one of the lightest reds, top examples show layers of strawberry, raspberry, plum, and dark forest fruits, with aromas of earth, spice, animal, cedar, and truffle. These wines range from delicate and minerally to silky and rich. Try those from the Côte de Nuits (Burgundy), and New Zealand's Central Otago and Martinborough regions.

Primitivo/Zinfandel
For ages we thought these were different varieties, but they're actually the same. Zinfandel ("Zin" for short) is found in the mighty USA, where most things big are seen as beautiful. In southern Italy, Primitivo rides high alongside Negroamaro and Nero d'Avola. With plenty of sweet, ripe fruit and aromas of violets and leather, this style is much more restrained than its transatlantic brother.

Rioja (ree-O-hah)
Rioja is a wine region in northern Spain best known for its rich, full-flavoured reds. Tempranillo is the star grape of Rioja, although red varieties Garnacha, Graciano, and Mazuelo are also permitted in the blend. Similarly, as a changing of the guard takes place in the region, international varieties such as Cabernet Sauvignon, Merlot, and Syrah are finding their way into Rioja's modern face with increasing frequency.

Rosé (rose-AY)
Rosé is a style of wine. It can be made sweet, dry, or anywhere in between. It can be made from just about any grape, and can come from pretty much anywhere. There are a couple of ways to make rosé. The first is to take a finished white wine and then back-blend it with some finished red. The second, and most common, way is using the *saignée* method. This is a bit like making a cup of tea, and involves leaving the skins in contact with the juice for a period of time (anywhere from a few hours to a couple of days) to get the desired level of colour, flavour, and tannin. The wine is then fermented as though it were a white wine.

Sangiovese (*san-gee-o-VAY-zay*)

Loaded with aromas of dark cherry, plum, and forest fruits, Sangiovese often also smells of tobacco, spice, and earth. Most remember its trademark "super-drying" tannins, which, without food, can make this grape a hard slog. It's native to Tuscany, where it shines as Chianti Classico and Brunello di Montalcino. More recently, it has surfaced in both Australia and the USA, but so far without the same success.

Syrah/Shiraz (*SIH-rah/SHEER-az*)

Syrah is the French name for this grape. It is lighter in body than Shiraz, with aromas of redcurrants, raspberry, plum, and nearly always white pepper and spice. Shiraz, from Australia and the New World, tends to be concentrated and ripe. At its best, it oozes plum, raspberry, earth, cedar, and freshly ground black pepper. Some New World winemakers are now calling their wines Syrah to reflect the lighter style they are now making.

Tempranillo (*tem-pra-NEE-yo*)

The grand old man of Spanish wine. Native to Rioja, it has also sunk its roots in nearby Ribera del Duero, Navarra, Priorat, and Toro. Typically, it has a solid core of dark berry fruits complete with a rustic edge that relies on savoury aromas such as tobacco, spice, leather, and earth. A recent trend has been to make international styles with big colour, big fruit, and big oak.

Touriga Nacional (*too-REE-ga nas-see-o-NAHL*)

Touriga plays a starring role in many of Portugal's great fortified wines as well as being an important component in more than a few of its new-wave table wines. Deep, densely fruited, leathery, and with an almost inky texture, Touriga needs time to mellow. Expect to smell things like dried fruit, leather, and violets, while fortified wines will be richer, stacked with dried-fruit flavour, and boasting plenty of sweetness.

The
Hot 100

Drink

Give

Dine

Splurge

Stash

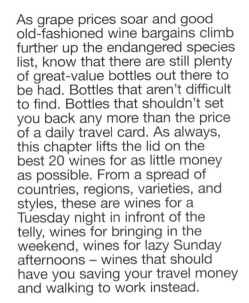

As grape prices soar and good old-fashioned wine bargains climb further up the endangered species list, know that there are still plenty of great-value bottles out there to be had. Bottles that aren't difficult to find. Bottles that shouldn't set you back any more than the price of a daily travel card. As always, this chapter lifts the lid on the best 20 wines for as little money as possible. From a spread of countries, regions, varieties, and styles, these are wines for a Tuesday night in infront of the telly, wines for bringing in the weekend, wines for lazy Sunday afternoons – wines that should have you saving your travel money and walking to work instead.

20 wines for drinking now

drink

Tesco Finest Bisol Prosecco VSAQ NV

Veneto
Italy

As Champagne prices continue skyward, the need for good-value and well-made sparkling wine has never been greater. From supermarket goliath Tesco, this is tidy, polished, and bone-dry Prosecco that amply ticks all the right boxes. If I sound excited, that's because I am, as up until not so long ago, good Prosecco was something of an oxymoron. Expect to find a compact wine concealing plenty of bright green apple and lemon sherbet character. In your mouth, a charge of tiny bubbles finishes things off nicely. Supermarkets will discount wines at certain times of the year so watch out for variations in price.

Yalumba Y Series Sangiovese Rosé 2007
Barossa Valley
Australia

Year in year out, Yalumba's Y Series wines provide some of the best-value examples of their kind. One of the more recent additions to the Y Series family is this snappy, dry rosé made from Italy's red grape superstar, Sangiovese. A short skin contact and cool fermentation have produced a fruity, fresh style that manages to exercise restraint where many others do not. Expect a nose of raspberries, redcurrants, and spice, while in your mouth this wine has terrific balance with sweet, dark fruit and a tight, structured finish.

Martin Sarmiento Mencía Bierzo 2005
Castilla y León
Spain

High up in Spain's Northwestern corner straddling the boarder of Galicia and Castilla y León is the increasingly fashionable region of El Bierzo. Red grape variety Mencía is the local star producing fresh, fruit-driven wines with bright acidity and dry, grippy tannins. In the case of this example, great old-vine fruit coupled with the Midas touch of winemaker Martin Sarmiento has produced a wine layered with cassis, cherry, smoke, and spice. A short stint in oak has provided ample backbone and balance.

get it from...

£8.99

Waitrose
C & D Wines

Chapoutier Organic Côtes du Rhône 2007

Southern Rhône
France

Exclusive to Waitrose, Michelle Chapoutier's Organic Côtes du Rhône remains one of the wine world's great bargains. As one of the best-known names in France's Rhône Valley, Chapoutier practice organic and biodynamic viticulture wherever possible – and for a company of this size, that is no small undertaking. Grenache and Syrah make up this elegant and spicy blend from a great Southern Rhône vintage. Expect bright, red-berried fruit and spice on the nose, while the palate is medium-bodied, fresh, and dry.

Georges Duboeuf
Beaujolais-Villages 2007

Burgundy
France

Beaujolais is the all-terrain wine style that you can definitely pair with fish, confidently drink alongside a range of spicy foods, and happily toss into the fridge without guilt. One-hundred per cent Gamay, picked from the high-altitude vineyards around the village of Chiroubles, this straightforward, light, and easy-drinking red from the self-proclaimed "King of Beaujolais" provides super-value summer sipping. Bright and explosive with zero oak influence, expect aromas of sweet cherry, violet, and musk, while in your mouth it's soft and juicy with fresh acidity and fine, slinky tannin.

get it from...

£7.99–8.99

Tesco (www.tesco.com only)
Majestic Wine Warehouse
Thresher
Berkmann Wine
   Cellars

Telmo Rodriguez
Al Muvedre 2007
Rueda
Spain

The Telmo Rodriguez approach is not an uncommon one: respect the past, believe in the future, do things as naturally as you can, intervene as little as possible, and let the identity of the place speak for itself via the finished product. From the tiny Valencian DO of Alicante, Al Muvedre is a down-to-earth, young, unoaked red designed to be drunk now. Aromas range from dark-berried fruits through to smoke, earth, and ground dried spice. There's good weight on the palate also, where after a wash of sweet cherry fruit a wave of fine, chewy tannins finishes things off.

Supermarket sweep

Something phenomenal has taken place in my local supermarket. Not quite an act of God, but by supermarket standards, not far off. It involves the natural food section, you know, that skinny little section sandwiched in between dried goods and gift cards – the section more commonly associated with dreadlocks, tie-dye clothes, and hand-made leather things. Well, in my supermarket that section is seriously on the shrink.

But before you start jumping up and down on your couch shouting things like "stinking hippies", "take that", and "I told you it wouldn't last", you should probably know that the natural foods section is only shrinking because it can no longer contain the sheer volume of naturally produced groceries coming onto the market, and nor can it keep up with consumer demand. Natural foods are taking over my supermarket shelves, and I reckon that's a really good thing.

Organic culture is everywhere. Once a word you simply filed in between alfalfa and yoga, organics have infiltrated all things consumable, wine included, and have quickly become a mainstream way of life. By definition, organic wines are those produced from grapes grown without the use of industrial fertilizers, herbicides, fungicides, pesticides, and excluding the addition of synthetic additives. Given our rising curiosity for knowing more about what we eat and drink, organic farming is a natural and responsible practice via which many of the world's greatest wines are produced. The growing number of great-value examples hitting the shelves is better news still.

£4.99

Waitrose
Constellation

Mezzomondo Negroamaro Rosso Salento 2006
Puglia
Italy

There's a whole lot to love about this value-packed Puglise red from the southeastern sub-region of Salento, otherwise known as "the heel" in Italy's boot. With Negroamaro (black bitter) as the star of the show, expect to find a nose flooded with black-berried fruit, liquorice, and Coca-Cola smells, while in your mouth it's flavour packed, soft, a little bit chewy, and utterly delicious. At this price, is there a better partner to Friday night pizza? Surely not.

De Bortoli Gulf Station Pinot Noir 2007
Yarra Valley
Australia

BARGAIN OF THE YEAR

PRODUCER OF THE YEAR

Remembering we're not talking about a variety that's cheap to produce, De Bortoli Gulf Station Pinot Noir – sourced entirely from Yarra Valley fruit – is really exceptional value for money. With Steve Webber and Young Australian Winemaker of the Year, Bill Downie, at the controls, this is great Pinot with terrific balance and intensity. Cherry red to look at, expect a nose loaded with sweet dark fruit, earth, and sweet spices such as cinnamon, nutmeg, and clove. The palate shows great varietal definition with brilliant intensity of flavour and a wash of fine, silky tannins.

get it from...

£9.99–11.49

Sainsbury's
Oddbins
De Bortoli UK

Rio Sol Vale do Sao Francisco Brazil Red 2006

Pernambuco
Brazil

Defying Mother Nature, Rio Sol sources fruit grown in the Vale do Sao Francisco region on the eighth parallel south of the equator. Make no mistake, this is hot, dry, harsh terrain, but – having already chalked up a bronze medal at the *Decanter* World Wine Awards and 83/100 from *Wine Spectator* – it's an impressive start. Cabernet Sauvignon and Shiraz form a compact nose of dark-plum, cherry, and smoked meat, while a dry, full, and soft mouthful of wine offers great value-for-money and an exciting glimpse into Brazil's future in wine.

get it from...

£4.99

Waitrose
Oakley Wine Agencies

Plantagenet
Omrah Shiraz 2005
Mount Barker
Australia

Plantaganet is regarded by many not just as one of Western Australia's top producers, but one of Australia's. Estate grown and produced wines are bottled under the Plantaganet label, while the "Omrah" range relies on top-quality fruit from around the state. Think sweet black cherries, wood smoke, and pepper, which just about jump all over you thanks to a small addition of Viognier. Take a slurp and find a full, seamless palate with plenty of dark fruit and great balance.

get it from...

£9.95

Andrew Chapman Fine Wines
Nickolls & Perks
Valvona & Crolla
Liberty Wines

Nothing fancy, just somewhere cool, dark, and vibration free. If you've got a few good bottles stashed away under the hot water service, on top of the fridge, or next to the fireplace: what are you thinking? Do the right thing and look after them properly.

Build yourself a cellar

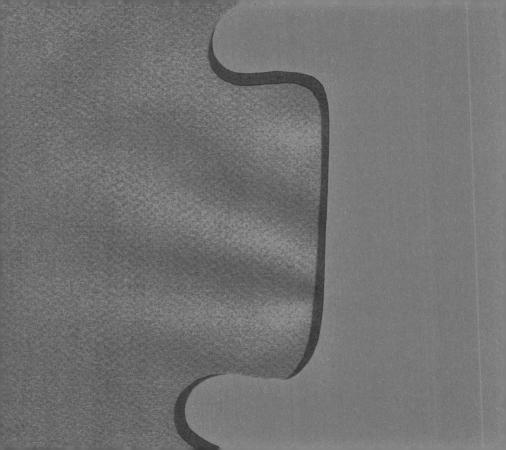

Hugel Gentil 2006
Alsace
France

Once upon a time in the fairytale-like villages of Alsace, all wines produced from a blend of noble grape varieties were labelled as "Gentil". Hugel's version continues the tradition, bringing together the noble (but slightly uncool) five-some of Gewurztraminer, Pinot Gris, Riesling, Muscat, and Sylvaner. The result is as exotic as the blend suggests, with aromas of jasmine, rose, clementine, and musk dominating the nose. The palate falls somewhere between medium- and full-bodied and, above all, is beautifully balanced..

£6.99

Waitrose
Liberty Wines

Monteforte
Soave Classico 2006
Veneto
Italy

Dividing his time between Italy and
New Zealand, Matt Thomson produces
a clean, pure snapshot of Soave from
Italy's northeast. Produced from
100 per cent Garganega and with zero
oak influence, you can expect a light,
delicate, fruit-forward wine with a
pretty nose of green apple, pear, and
honeysuckle. In the mouth it's super
fresh and perfectly suited to simply
grilled fish, new spring greens, and
a squeeze of lemon.

Torres
Viña Esmeralda 2007
Penedès
Spain

Viña Esmeralda is a dry and flamboyantly aromatic blend of Moscatel and Gewurztraminer that's been souped-up with a splash of Riesling. For a small amount of money you get a huge amount of personality in return. With zero oak influence, you can expect to find on the nose a pretty mixture of jasmine, musk, and lychee, while in your mouth this wine is crisp – nowhere near as rich as you might expect – and beautifully balanced. Just the kind of thing you would expect from Torres: one of the world's great exponents of great value drinking.

get it from...

£6.99

Tesco
Waitrose (www.waitrosewine.com only)
Oddbins
Booths
J E Fells & Sons

Marks & Spencer Tupungato Chardonnay 2007
Mendoza
Argentina

In an effort to woo a new audience, and reassure an old one, Chardonnay has had a long overdue makeover. Gone is the heavy-handed use of oak and the super-sized tropical fruit and in its place is a leaner, more focused style of Chardonnay that's not only better balanced, but better suited to food, too. From the stables of Argentinian superstars Catena, this example – exclusive to M&S – is not just a great example of Chardonnay's new breed, but an incredible buy at this price.

get it from...
£6.99

Marks & Spencer

Dr Loosen "L" Riesling 2007
Mosel
Germany

With holdings throughout Germany's most famed vineyards, together with ecologically sound and sustainable practices, Ernie Loosen is widely regarded as one of finest exponents of Riesling anywhere in the world. His most basic offering is a delicate and attractive wine that walks the tightrope between sweetness and acidity with ease. Combining aromas of jasmine, mandarin, spice, and lime, it boasts a racy palate that pulls up just this side of dry. This is a stunning example from one of Germany's top producers.

get it from...

£6.99

Sainsbury's
Booths
Oddbins
Great Western Wine
D Byrne & Co
ABS Wine Agencies

get it from...

£9.99

Noel Young Wines
Vin du Vin
Highbury Vintners
The Guildford Wine Company
Abbey Wines
Peter Lehmann UK

Peter Lehmann
Eden Valley Riesling 2007
Eden Valley
Australia

The Eden Valley is renowned for producing a tight, steely, and firmly structured style of Riesling that has a serious capacity to age. Less fashionable than the nearby Clare Valley, good examples are readily available and remain some of Australia's great-value wine buys. Having scooped a bag of awards, this example from Peter Lehmann is right on the money. From its piercing nose of fresh lime juice and spring flowers, to its intense and angular palate, this is simply one of the year's great wine bargains.

Stella Bella
Sauvignon Blanc 2008
Margaret River
Australia

Margaret River in Western Australia produces – alongside the country's most finely tuned offerings of Cabernet Sauvignon – some of Australia's most deliciously drinkable examples of Sauvignon Blanc. And while we think Janice McDonald's racy blend of Sem/Sauv is perhaps a better addition to the dinner table, it certainly hasn't stopped us from giving away multiple bottles of her delicious Sauvignon Blanc as tokens of appreciation. Pristine, pale, fresh as a daisy, and loaded with passion fruit, blackcurrant, fresh spring herb and mineral character, this is mouthwatering Sauvignon Blanc from one of Western Australia's brightest stars.

get it from...

£9.99

The Wine Society
Ann et Vin
Vinology
The Sampler

Earth, wind, and fire

Imagine I told you that in order to make biodynamic wine you'd have to fill a cow's horn with manure, bury it approximately 40–60cm (15–23 in) underground in the autumn, and unearth it the following spring. You'd think I was nuts, right? Imagine I went on to tell you that the horn's contents would replace any conventional herbicides, pesticides, and fungicides that you would otherwise normally use to protect your vines against all kinds of nasty stuff, and that much of your work both in the vineyard and the winery would take place in line with the various phases of the moon – oh yeah – and naked… You'd be convinced I was either having you on, or totally off my rocker.

Rather complicated and highly controversial, biodynamic farming is the brainchild of German philosopher Rudolph Steiner.

Steiner was primarily concerned with bridging the gap between the material and the physical, and toward the end of his life, he applied his spiritual science of "anthroposophy" to agriculture.

With elements of homeopathy, astronomy, and astrology, biodynamics looks at the entire vineyard and everything in it. It's about creating a balanced and healthy eco-system, taking into consideration flora, fauna, soil fertility, and crop nutrition.

Confused? Relax, you wouldn't be alone. Even some of the biodynamic movement's biggest supporters – which include some of the world's most respected wine producers – aren't totally sure of how it works either, although all agree unanimously that their vines have never been healthier, and their wines have never tasted better.

get it from...

£7.45

The Sussex Wine Company
Enotria Winecellars

Umani Ronchi Villa Bianchi Verdicchio 2007
Umbria
Italy

As more and more wine drinkers are looking to Italy's raft of great but hugely underappreciated whites for an increasing number of food-friendly, great-value wines, this simple yet beautifully made example of one of Italy's more interesting white grapes, Verdicchio, is well worth a look. Packing tart green apple, pear, honeysuckle, and plenty of citrus zip and zing, Umani Ronchi's entry level Verdicchio, Villa Bianchi, is a brilliant introduction to Italian white wine from one of Umbria's star estates.

Cono Sur Viognier 2008
Bío Bío Valley
Chile

Native to France's Northern Rhône
Valley, Viognier has certainly covered
some ground in recent years. Having
made headway in Australia, North
America, South Africa – and even a
cameo appearance in Thailand – this
example hails from Chile's cool-climate
wine capital, the Bío-Bío Valley.
Displaying serious freshness and
charm, a big sniff reveals aromas of
apricot, orange peel, and fresh spring
flowers, while just a hint of oak – for
complexity rather than influence –
sets the tone for a soft, rich mouthful.

get it from...

£6.99

Majestic Wine Warehouse
Somerfield
Waitrose

The wine section of any supermarket can be a frightening place, but it can also be the source of some great bargains – some of the best value lies in lesser known countries, varieties, regions, and styles. You might have to look a little harder to find them, but it'll be worth it.

Escape your comfort zone

Laroche Chablis 2006
Burgundy
France

Classically styled and beautifully made, this is pristine Chablis from one of the region's most innovative stars. As some of the most pure expressions of Chardonnay you can find, wines from the Laroche stable tend towards being squeaky clean, mineral in texture, and often void of any oak influence. Aromas and flavours range from lemon and honey through hay to chalk. This, Michel Laroche's basic Chablis, is a fine example from the highly regarded 2006 vintage.

get it from...

£8.99

Tesco
Asda
Bibendum

You've got a new girlfriend, maybe a pay rise from the boss is on the cards, perhaps you're meeting the "in-laws to be" for the very first time, you're off to dinner with friends (who know a thing or two about wine), you forgot your dad's birthday, you need to make an apology, a bribe – perhaps it's for love, maybe its for money, it might even be for both – whatever the reason the following 20 wines are guaranteed to make even the most buttoned-up of wine connoisseurs go fuzzy. These are the 20 wines you should be giving this year.

20 wines for putting smiles on faces

give

Lanson Black Label NV
Champagne
France

Lets face it: who doesn't like getting a bottle of Champagne? A few moons have past since I last gave Lanson's universally loved Black Label a proper go. I wish I had sooner – I'd have saved myself a lot of money. At a smidge over £25, this is simply one of the best-value non-vintage Champagnes around. Richer than I remembered, expect a nose full of ripe citrus, fresh bread, pretty Pinot fruit, and spice. The palate has terrific drive and intensity, all of which is bound up by lots of stylish little bubbles and a long, balanced finish. Give it with pride.

get it from...

£25.50

Tesco
Sainsbury's
Waitrose
Bibendum
Lanson UK

Yarra Burn
Pinot Noir / Chardonnay / Pinot Meunier Brut 2005
Yarra Valley
Australia

Established in 1975 in the foothills of Victoria's Warburton Ranges, Yarra Burn is a pioneer of Yarra Valley sparkling wine production. The first vintage of Yarra Burn sparkling was released in 1983. Nowadays, Ed Carr – perhaps the greatest sparkling winemaker outside of Champagne – is responsible not only for production, but also for the impressive haul of accolades this wine has collected over the years. Expect a compact and clean nose of tart green apples, citrus, toasted brioche, and spice, thanks to extended time on lees. In your mouth there's terrific intensity of ripe lemony fruit, a wash of fine bubbles, and a long, clean finish. Have a couple on standby.

get it from...

£12.99

Wine Studio
Constellation

They'll make all the difference. Avoid fancy colours, patterns, and shapes: the best glasses are clear, have a tear-drop-shaped bowl that's wider at the bottom than top, and a stem. Durability is really important, too, and while hand-made, lead-crystal glasses are lovely to drink out of, they're not necessarily the most practical for everyday use.

Buy some decent glasses

Taylor's LBV 2002
Douro
Portugal

Established in 1692, Taylor's was the first British port firm to buy vineyards in the Douro Valley. Taylor's Late Bottled Vintage (LBV) range – wines that have already spent four years in oak – are without question some of the best of their kind. This wine is no exception. Unfiltered and having been matured for a further five years prior to release, this is concentrated and power-packed port with a nose of dried fig, dark plum, and bitter chocolate. In your mouth it's inky and rich with masses of intensity and a clean, well-balanced finish – the perfect Christmas give.

get it from...

£11.99

Tesco
Sainsbury's
Waitrose
Majestic Wine Warehouse
Mentzendorff

Keep it in the closet

We don't like to talk about it, yet most blokes will agree that there's nothing quite like a week on the beach to remind you that you're not getting any younger. From the indignity of having to squeeze your love handles into last year's board shorts, to the realization that your pecks have now fully blossomed into man boobs – it's all a stark reminder that you're not what you used to be. Similarly, not all wine gets better with age, and those that do can often attribute their longevity to the grape variety/varieties used, the country and region of origin, the method of production, and how the wine was stored.

For most of us, the idea of starting a cellar is about as much a priority as starting next year's tax return. After all, aren't cellars just for the well heeled – for the really hardcore wine enthusiasts – the sacred domain of those who persist in wearing bow-ties despite the fact that they went out of fashion two decades ago? No. You don't need to know much about wine to have a cellar. And your cellar can be as basic as a simple stack of cardboard boxes in the corner of a room, or on a grander scale, cellars can be state-of-the-art, blinged-out, cavernous underground spaces.

The point is that, if you have more than just a few decent bottles lying around, then you should look after them properly, and that means finding somewhere cool, dark, vibration-free – and preferably somewhere with a lock.

get it from...

£9.50

Berry Bros & Rudd
WoodWinters Wines & Whiskies
Fields, Morris & Verdin

Domaine de Triennes Vin Gris Coteaux Varois 2007
Provence
France

From Burgundy legend Jacques Seysses, Domaine de Triennes Vin Gris is stylish, estate-grown rosé from the outskirts of Aix-en-Provence. The vineyards are farmed meticulously, incorporating a mix of organic and biodynamic principles, while the production process is two-fold and begins with a lightning-fast three-hour skin contact before a cool, month-long fermentation. The result is a pale and attractive mouthwatering blend of Cinsault, Syrah, and Merlot – from which you can expect to find a nose crammed with raspberry, redcurrant, and dried herbs, while a fresh, fruit-driven palate gives way to crunchy acidity and a clean, drying finish.

£10.99

Majestic Wine Warehouse
PLB Group Ltd

Fuentespina Crianza 2005
Ribera del Duero
Spain

Bodega Avelino Vegas is a small cooperative producing wines from Rioja, Rías Baixas, Castilla y León, and Rueda, and includes Ribera del Duero-based Bodega Fuentespina. With close to 300 hectares (741 acres) of vines at an average age of 25 years, Fuentespina produces a modern style of Tempranillo with an emphasis on value for money – something of an anomaly in modern Ribera del Duero. Labelled *crianza* (kree-AN-zah) – reference to its one year in tank and one in oak before release – dark cherry and forest fruits add balance to an attractive rustic nose. The palate is well knit, medium in body, and a wash of drying tannins closes things nicely.

Porcupine Ridge Syrah / Viognier 2007
Franschhoek
South Africa

From the stables of Boekenhoutskloof and the hands of Marc Kent – one of South Africa's top estates and one of its most talented winemakers – Porcupine Ridge remains one of the country's star buys and highlights just how good the Western Cape can be at entry level. Co-fermented Syrah and Viognier (with more than just a glancing nod to the Northern Rhône) combine to produce an opulent nose of sweet black cherry, pepper, ripe apricot, and spice. Oak is dealt out sparingly and comes courtesy of top-notch, two-year-old French barrels, while the palate is rich, broad, and finely structured.

McHenry Hohnen
3 Amigos GSM 2006
Margaret River
Australia

Having established Cape Mentelle in 1970 and the iconic Cloudy Bay in 1985, McHenry Hohnen is David Hohnen's latest venture that – together with daughter, Freya, and brother-in-law, Murray McHenry – produces a range of grape varieties and wine styles from four vineyards that employ "great grandpa farming". This is based on the idea that long before modern chemicals and synthetic additives, farmers worked to create a naturally balanced eco-system in order to get the best from their land. From the range, 3 Amigos GSM is a soft drink-now blend of Grenache, Shiraz, and Mataro, where dark fruit and lovely Rhône-inspired spice lead you to a palate that is plush and full of bright berry fruit.

get it from...

£10.99

Harvey Nichols
S H Jones
Cheviot Wine Agencies
Lakeland Vintners
Louis Latour UK

MontGras
Carmenère Reserva 2006
Colchagua
Chile

get it from...

£6.99

Waitrose
Enotria Winecellars

Former Old-World resident, Carmenère, has found new life in the sun-drenched vineyards of Chile. Bearing an uncanny likeness to Merlot, the best examples are beautifully balanced and ooze sweet, ripe fruit. Colchagua Valley-based Viña MontGras produce one of Chile's best examples. Grapes are harvested by hand, while fermentation takes place in temperature-controlled stainless-steel tanks. Sixty per cent of the wine is then aged for seven months in French and American oak (40/60). Expect sweet dark plum, violet, and ground coffee on the nose, while in the mouth it's full and firm with soft chewy tannins to finish. The perfect give for those who prefer their reds on the bigger side.

De Bortoli Yarra Valley Pinot Noir 2006
Yarra Valley
Australia

PRODUCER OF THE YEAR

With Steve Webber and Bill Downie at the controls – two of Australia's most exciting winemakers – it isn't difficult to understand the buzz around De Bortoli's Yarra Valley outpost. Over the past decade all its vineyards have been re-graded according to quality, there has been a definite nod towards organic practices, vineyards have been re-orientated to reduce sun exposure, and hands have been favoured over machines. The same attitude extends to the winery where, along with stricter sorting, no cultured yeasts are used during fermentation and older oak is favoured over new. The result is lush, smooth, and elegant Pinot that any lover of top drawer Pinot Noir will appreciate.

get it from...

£15.99–17.99

Oddbins
Averys Wine Merchants
R S Wines Ltd
De Bortoli UK

Bell Hill
Old Weka Pass Road
Pinot Noir 2006
Canterbury
New Zealand

Long before Bell Hill Pinot Noir got wine-lovers around the planet frothing at the mouth with excitement – me included – Old Weka Pass Road was the first example of this variety produced by Marcel Giesen and Sherwyn Veldhuizen at their Canterbury estate. From a selection of limestone-rich vineyards with high-density planting and a mixture of clones, this is multi-layered and purely fruited Pinot Noir that is slightly animal, mineral in texture, extremely seductive, slinky, fine, and, most of all, worth every single penny. Oak is dealt out sparingly with the wine spending 12 months in French barrels, only 25 per cent of which are new.

get it from...

£24.49

Wheeler Cellars
Lay & Wheeler

£7.99

Waitrose
Negociants UK

Yalumba Organic Shiraz 2006
Barossa Valley
Australia

Last year Yalumba was acknowledged by the US Environmental Protection Agency for its efforts in eco-system management, for building an energy efficient winery, and producing 98 per cent of packaging from recyclable materials, but not least of all, for allocating 55 hectares (135 acres) of prime land to preserving local wildlife – land that could have been used to plant vines. And on that note, this is delicious and great-value Shiraz that, complete with its sweet, plummy core, spice-driven nose, plush mouth-feel, great intensity, and a wash of dry grainy tannins, effortlessly ticks all the right boxes.

Mount Langi Ghiran
Cliff Edge Shiraz 2002
Central Victoria
Australia

While the flagship wine from this estate consistently ranks as one of the top examples of Shiraz produced in Australia, its younger sibling, "Cliff Edge", is certainly no slouch. Drawing on fruit sourced from a precariously positioned vineyard at the base of a 540m (1,770ft) cliff, and from a selection of small local growers, Cliff Edge is an essay in power, style, and finesse. Dark and inky colour leads you to a nose that's sweet, juicy, and packed with aromas of blood plum, dark cherry, blackcurrant, ground coffee, chocolate, pepper, and spice. In the mouth it's sweet, dense, and chewy, with plenty of dark fruit and well-handled, spicy French oak.

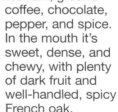

Sonoma-Cutrer Chardonnay 2006
Sonoma
USA

There are few places into which Chardonnay hasn't sunk its roots. It's been a big winner in the New World, and has developed a real affinity with California's Napa Valley. But, where a lot of California Chardonnay is overenthusiastically super-sized with a double helping of oak, Sonoma-Cutrer Chardonnay is intense and full-fruited, managing to retain real charm and character at the same time. From its tightly packed and intense nose of grapefruit, cashew, and hazelnut to its finely structured palate, this is a first-class lesson in how good New World Chardonnay can, and should, be. Give it to the doubters.

Up and away (Part I)

"And how many bags will you be checking in today Mr Skinner?"

"Just the two," I replied.

"I'm afraid Mr Skinner any more than one will incur an additional charge of £95 (AUS$195) per bag."

Cue major jaw drop. "Why?"

But I didn't need an explanation, I knew why. This was the airline industry – the world's biggest carbon polluter – taking the initiative to offset emissions through excess baggage. Brilliant idea: I could hardly hand over my credit card fast enough.

"What do you do with the money," I asked. "Plant trees?"

"Oh no Mr Skinner, this has nothing to do with the environment – it's a baggage handlers' fee to help cover overtime. Now if you'd kindly sign here please…"

Bugger.

The planet is suffering, and while grape-growers get greener by the minute, the rest of the wine industry (which stands to feel the effects of environmental change before most) is slowly catching on. Spanish wine giant Torres is swapping over an entire fleet of company cars. "Toyota Prius for everyone," says Miguel Torres proudly – a move set to reduce the company's carbon output by around 1,000 tones per year.

Over in Oz, Yalumba have just been acknowledged by the US Environmental Protection Agency for their environmental approach to winemaking (*see page 75*).

It may not sound like much, but it's a start.

Thandi Fairtrade Chardonnay 2007
Elgin Valley
South Africa

Fairtrade was set up in order to guarantee that disadvantaged producers in the developing world were getting a better deal. From the moment you arrive at Thandi, there is an obvious sense of pride and passion that radiates from all involved. And proud all involved should be, as in 1993 Thandi were the first ever winery to achieve Fairtrade accreditation. Thandi Chardonnay is everything I'd hope to see from great – even pricier – New World examples: ripe stone fruit, well-used oak, textural, long, and balanced. Give it as often as you can.

Stella Bella Semillon / Sauvignon Blanc 2008
Margaret River
Australia

Making its second appearance in *The Juice*, Stella Bella Semillon/Sauvignon Blanc 2008 from the hands of Western Australia-great, Janice McDonald, is yet another stylish example of this much-loved Margaret River blend – and the latest in a long line of excellent offerings from this estate. Assembled from roughly two parts Semillon for its weight, purity, and focus and one part Sauvignon Blanc for freshness, zip, and vibrancy, expect a beautifully knit, full-flavoured, long, crisp, and crunchy dry white wine perfectly geared for everyday drinking. If the sun happens to be shining in your corner of the world, then this is the wine to give.

d'Arenberg Hermit Crab Viognier / Marsanne 2006
McLaren Vale
Australia

With the Gulf of Saint Vincent a mere hop, skip, and jump away from McLaren Vale, the calcareous remains of many fossilized creatures from the deep – including the hermit crab – make up the limestone base upon which many of the region's vines are planted. Having done an about-face on the blend – Viognier and Marsanne rather than Marsanne and Viognier – Hermit Crab is full and generous with an exotic nose of apricot, orange blossom, and jasmine. In the mouth, trademark Viognier weight is underlined beautifully by Marsanne's zip and freshness, and only one-third of the blend sees time in old oak.

get it from...

£7.59–8.49

Waitrose
Oddbins
Bibendum

Fairleigh Estate Chardonnay 2006
Marlborough
New Zealand

With its carpet of vines, snow-capped peaks, emerald-coloured rivers, rolling green mountains, and air so fresh it hurts, Marlborough – occupying the northern tip of New Zealand's South Island – is home to one of the world's most distinctive wine styles. But, beyond Sauvignon Blanc, there are other things grown in Marlborough, notably Chardonnay. From Fairleigh Estate, expect to find a nose of honeysuckle, pear, river rock, and cashew, while the palate is rich with soft stone fruit and bright mineral texture. The result is a restrained yet beautifully crafted wine that represents outstanding value for money.

get it from...
£7.49

Majestic Wine Warehouse

Which doesn't necessarily mean shelling out. If you never spend any more than £5 (AUS$10) on a bottle of wine, by spending £6 (AUS$12) – even by stretching that little further – in theory fixed production costs stay the same and what increases is the value of the liquid in the bottle, meaning the quality of what you're drinking stands to markedly improve.

Trade up

Fiano di Avellino dei Feudi di San Gregorio 2007

Campania
Italy

get it from...

£9.99

Waitrose
Enotria

As Italy's winemaking south continues to gain major kudos, a handful of lesser-known white grapes from the chilly hills of Campania continue to raise eyebrows. Established in 1986, Feudi di San Gregorio has grown to become one of the region's top producers. Its fruit is sourced from a mix of estate-grown and bought-in grapes, while direction in the winery is left up to Riccardo Cottarella. This is green/gold Fiano complete with aromas of lemon sherbet, lime, and fennel. The palate is spotless and fresh with not a hint of oak in sight, while pure citrus fruit builds to make way for a tight, dry finish.

£7.99

Hedley Wright
Whitebridge Wines Ltd
Field & Fawcett
   Wine Merchants
    & Delicatessen
The World of Wine
Stevens Garnier

Wirra Wirra Scrubby Rise Sauvignon Blanc / Semillon / Viognier 2008

McLaren Vale
Australia

The trio of Sauvignon Blanc (45 per cent), Semillon (39 per cent), and odd-man-out Viognier (16 per cent) unite here to form one of the planet's best-value dry white wines. Bizarrely, the vineyard of the same name – from which a large chunk of the Semillon component is taken – is pretty much flat and scrubless. Anyway, calling on fruit from McLaren Vale, Fleurieu Peninsula, and the chilly Adelaide Hills, a big sniff will reveal classic grapefruit, gooseberry, and mineral character, while the palate is dry, broad, and balanced beautifully by mouthwatering acidity and great length of flavour. Great for giving, but just as good for keeping.

£10.95

Waitrose
Wine in Cornwall
Wadebridge Wines
Camel Valley Winery

Camel Valley Bacchus 2006
Cornwall
England

A mix of the right varieties, the right sites, (God forbid) global warming, and most importantly, a level of local expertise that has never been as high, has resulted in a handful of world-class and award-winning English wines. Camel Valley is situated on the slopes above the River Camel – halfway between the Atlantic and English Channel coasts and just a few miles from Bodmin. Plus, just in case you were wondering, Bacchus is the love child of (Silvaner x Riesling) x Müller-Thurgau and produces light, fresh, aromatic whites that have a distinctive herbal edge not dissimilar to Sauvignon Blanc.

Eat, drink, and be merry. That's what this chapter is about. This is the chapter where we lift the lid on 20 great food and wine combinations – 20 great wines that, no matter how bad you are in the kitchen, are guaranteed to bring smiles to faces. This isn't rocket science, and nor do you need to be an expert. Some of the best combinations are also some of the cheapest and easiest to reproduce. And, whether you choose to follow the rules or break them all, at the very heart of it, good food-and-wine matching knits a little bit of art with a little bit of science, and a lot of trial and error. Practice makes perfect? Bon Appetite!

20 wines to drink with food

dine

Jansz Premium Cuvée NV

Tasmania
Australia

The legendary soft-shell crab at Vietnamese restaurant Song Que (134 Kingsland Road, London E2 8DY) arrives lightly coated in a dry batter and tossed through a mixture of garlic, sea salt, and fresh chilies. It's a tough ask for most wines, although good sparkling wine is an obvious choice, and the Pipers River region in Tasmania is home to some of Australia's best. Of those, the much-loved Jansz packs a bright and clean nose of green apple, citrus, bread, and honey, then in your mouth great flavour and masses of bright tiny bubbles are all you'll need to navigate even the trickiest of tricky food textures.

Marks & Spencer Prosecco VSAQ Extra Dry NV
Veneto
Italy

Going a long way to prove that some of the greatest food and wine matches are also some of the easiest to create, the combination of Parmesan cheese and Prosecco is a pretty hard one to beat. A drizzle of really good honey will add to the magic, but it's pretty good as it is. This example from Loris Bonotto and exclusive to M&S, has plenty to offer. Expect aromas of ripe pear, Golden Delicious apples, and fresh grape juice; in your mouth the wine is intense and well balanced with lots of tiny bubbles to clean it up on the finish.

get it from...

£7.99

Marks & Spencer

La Gitana Manzanilla NV
Jerez
Spain

The best examples of manzanilla are bone dry, slightly nutty, and have a lovely salty tang – perfect for sparking your appetite. As a result, these wines truly rise to the occasion when paired with foods such as salty green olives, fresh or jarred anchovies, caperberries, cured meats, and nuts. From the seaside town of Sanlúcar de Barrameda, this is a cracking wine that represents outstanding value for money. Pale in colour, bone dry, and with its trademark salty tang, serve cold and you'll be hard pressed to find a better food wine on the planet.

get it from...

£7.99

Majestic Wine Warehouse
Sainsbury's
Tesco
Waitrose

Artadi Artazuri Garnacha Rosado 2006
Navarra
Spain

No longer just a summer standby, as food-friendly wine styles go, rosé (or *rosado*) ranks right up there with the best of them. Combine the freshest mozzarella you can lay your hands on, a couple of small, sweet tomatoes, and a drizzle of good olive oil for one of the best – and easiest – matches for light, dry rosé you can make. From Rioja's great Artadi, this wine from the 1996 venture into Navarra is pure class. From its pretty pink colour to its compact and fresh nose of wild raspberry, apple, and dried flowers, winemaker Juan Carlos Lopez de La Calle has fashioned this bone-dry *rosado* from 100 per cent Garnacha (or Grenache); it is bright, lively, and as good with food as it is just by itself.

A few things about Fairtrade and wine…

In 2003, a small community-run grape-growing/winemaking business in South Africa's Elgin Valley made history by becoming the first wine producer in the developing world to receive Faitrade accreditation. Their name, translating as "nurturing love", was Thandi.

Fairtrade came to the UK in 1992 in order to guarantee that disadvantaged producers in the developing world were getting a better deal. All Fairtrade products carry a symbol that can only be applied to products that have met criteria set out by Fairtrade standards. These standards cover things like paying prices to cover sustainable farming, paying premiums for community development, committing to partnerships that allow for long-term planning, and for

In 2007, just four years after Thandi received it's official accreditation, London played host to the Fairtrade wine committee's second annual wine tasting, where the number of Fairtrade-accredited wine producers – representing South Africa, Chile, and Argentina – had risen to 18. Eighteen producers who, in 2007 alone, managed to sell near enough to £8million (AUS$16.5million) – that's over 3.5 million litres (770,000 gallons) – worth of Fairtrade wine in the UK. Now that's impressive. Even more impressive is that since it's inception, sales of Fairtrade goods in the UK alone have exceeded £500million (AUS$1billion), which in turn has given around seven million people – farmers, workers, families – a shot at building a better future and the ability to compete more fairly in the global market place.

£12.95

Liberty Wines

S C Pannell "Pronto" 2007
McLaren Vale
Australia

You know it's been a good summer when, despite having sacrificed most of the hair on your arms and half an eyebrow to the barbeque, you managed to eat outdoors more than you ate in. The slick and affordable "Pronto" is a plush, drink now, all-terrain red from one of Australia's best winemakers, Steve Pannell. Assembled from old-vine McLaren Vale Grenache, Shiraz, and Touriga, expect plenty of sweet, dark fruit alongside a beautifully structured palate that has all you'll need to tackle even the toughest challenges the barbeque can dish up.

get it from...

£9.25

Majestic Wine Warehouse
The Wine Society
The Sampler
Vinum

Donnafugata
Sedàra IGT 2006
Sicily
Italy

Char-grilled, aged rib of beef rubbed with sea salt and finished with a decent slug of peppery olive oil needs wine with muscle and structure to match. To get to the point, you need a big gutsy red, and the under-appreciated Sicilian variety Nero d'Avola – with its weight, texture, and ripeness of fruit – is right up to the job. Sedàra is a clean, modern example sourced from lofty vineyards located at 300–400m (984–1,312ft) above sea level. With only half the wine spending between six to eight months in oak, expect a bright, fruit-driven nose of sweet, dark fruit and bitter chocolate, while a soft, juicy, and well-structured mouthful of wine completes the picture.

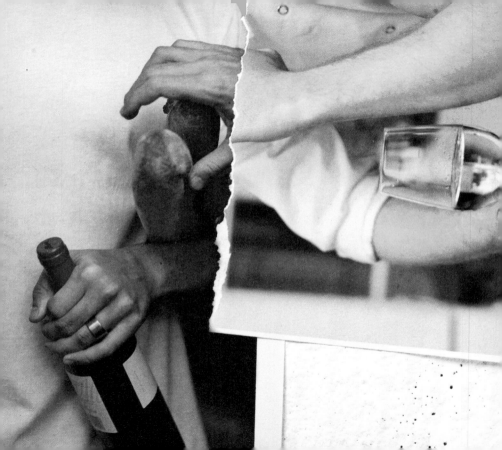

Poggiotondo Chianti Superiore DOCG 2006
Tuscany
Italy

If Friday night means pizza night in your house, then Sangiovese should be your first port of call. Aided by a small shot of Merlot, this is a quality example from the stables of renowned Tuscan consultant, Alberto Antonini. Having invested heavily in the regeneration of his family vineyards, Antonini has produced a modern style of Chianti that still manages to retain regional identity. Expect a nose of liqueur cherry, tobacco, and leather, while the not-so-typical Sangiovese palate shows off plenty of plush, ripe fruit and terrific balance between acid and tannin.

get it from...

£7.95

Andrew Chapman Fine Wines
Luvians Bottleshop
The Bottle Stop
The Fine Wine Company
The Secret Cellar
Whole Foods Market
Liberty Wines

Wild Rock
Gravel Pit Red 2006
Hawke's Bay
New Zealand

For a top Merlot food match, pound together a handful of coriander seeds, cumin seeds, a pinch of dried chili, and sea salt, before rubbing liberally into a boned half leg of lamb. Char-grill each side for ten minutes on a smoking-hot barbeque, letting it rest for a further ten minutes once done. And the wine? From a patch on the famed Gimblett Gravels vineyard area – that was nearly lost to a mining company some time back – this drink-now Merlot/Malbec blend is rich with dark, sweet plums, violets, roasting meat, and spice. In your mouth it's full and firm with dry, grippy tannins and all the style you'd expect from a relative of the great Craggy Range.

Cono Sur Pinot Noir 2008
Bío-Bío Valley
Chile

Along with our appetites, as the mercury rises over summer our tolerance for tannin-heavy reds all but disappears. This is a time of year for eating light. Think barbequed salmon, char-grilled tuna, pan-fried chicken, and then think Pinot Noir. Naturally light in tannin, this soft and delicious Pinot Noir is sourced from Colchagua in central Chile. Make no mistake, this is not top-end Pinot Noir, but with its sweet red fruit, exotic spice, and silky mouth-feel, this wine remains one of the world's best-value examples of this variety.

get it from...

£6.99

Tesco
Sainsbury's
Morrisons
Somerfield
Waitrose
Majestic Wine
    Warehouse

Viña Herminia
Rioja Crianza 2004
Rioja
Spain

This is the modern face of Rioja in full swing, complete with better colour, more layers on the nose, and a nicely structured palate. From 100 per cent Tempranillo that has spent little more than 12 months in a mixture of one- and two-year-old oak, expect to find masses of sweet black cherries, dried woody herbs, earth, and Middle Eastern spices, while in your mouth it is medium-bodied with plenty of drive and grip. Having already spent a few years in the bottle, age makes it ideal for drinking now. And think garlicky Middle Eastern meatballs with couscous, parsley, mint, preserved lemon, and almonds.

Ata Rangi Crimson Pinot Noir 2007
Martinborough
New Zealand

New Zealand – the cleanest, greenest country on earth – is also one of the wine world's most diverse. And, as Syrah and Merlot go from strength to strength up north, a fragile climate and poor soils provide an excellent starting point for Pinot Noir and a cast of whites in the south. At the southern end of the North Island, Martinborough produces some of the best examples of Pinot Noir outside of Burgundy. This example from the region's top producer is ripe, plush, stylish, and jammed full of seductive fruit and spice aromas; it offers a text-book silky mouth-feel and a long, fine finish.

Domaine de Durban Muscat de Beaumes-de-Venise 2006
Southern Rhône
France

get it from...

£12.95 (375ml)

Yapp Brothers
Berry Bros & Rudd

Like most grandmas, mine was certainly no slouch when it came to making puddings. Treacle tart was nearly always top of my request list, and hers to this day is only rivalled by those served up at St John restaurant (26 St John Street, London EC1M 4AY). And, while nan may have opted for a glass of sweet sherry, Muscat de Beaumes-de-Venise is well worth a look. Domaine de Durban is home to one of the finest examples produced in the Rhône. With zero botrytis influence, this is a clean, modern style where aromas of citrus marmalade, apricot, and pineapple dominate. In your mouth expect incredible length of flavour, a little alcoholic heat, and lovely bright acidity.

Lustau San Emilio Pedro Ximénez NV
Jerez
Spain

From Jerez in Spain's south, San Emilio Pedro Ximénez – from the hands of Lustau, one of Spain's greatest producers – has an intense nose of molasses, dried raisins, spice, and spirit, while in your mouth it's syrupy, rich, and long. Serve it alongside fruit cake or sticky toffee pudding, and that's almost as good as it gets. I say almost, because there is an easier alternative. This is an absolute no brainer and your guests or better half is going to love you for it! Grab a tub of rum and raisin ice cream (vanilla is just as good), place two scoops in a bowl and liberally pour the PX over the top as though it were chocolate sauce. And there you have it: an instant classic dessert.

£9.00 (375ml)

Fields, Morris & Verdin
The Wright Wine and Whisky Company
Whole Foods Market
The Vineking
Noel Young Wines

£14.99–15.99 (375ml)

Waitrose
Oddbins
Majestic Wine
    Warehouse
House of Fraser
Averys Wine
    Merchants
Hailsham Cellars
De Bortoli UK

De Bortoli Noble One 2005
Griffith
Australia

PRODUCER OF THE YEAR

Cheese fans take note: the next time you're offered a glass of port to go with your Stilton, politely decline and order yourself a glass of Australia's most famous sweet wine instead. Having won a swag of trophies, Noble One was born in 1982 via a bold and deliberate attempt to create a sweet wine from botrytis affected grapes. It remains one of Australia's most highly awarded and sought after wines. Expect a nose overflowing with ripe stone fruit, sweet orange marmalade, and spice, while the palate is bright and full – not cloying – with a long, crisp finish.

Flagstone Noon Gun White 2007
Somerset West
South Africa

get it from...

£7.99

Tesco
Constellation

My salad of last summer was char-grilled prawns, cucumber, mango, shallots, coriander, mint, and lime juice, and nine times out of ten Noon Gun was my wine. Bruce Jack is one of South Africa's most dynamic and forward-thinking producers – his Flagstone label offers serious value for money. Assembled from a motley mixture of 30 per cent Riesling, 30 per cent Chenin Blanc, 19 per cent Sauvignon Blanc, nine per cent Pinot Blanc, nine per cent barrel-fermented Chardonnay, and three per cent Sémillon, the Noon Gun explodes with ripe stone fruit and tropical fruit character on the nose, while in your mouth the sum of this wine's individual parts makes for a ripe, yet snappy, dry summer white.

As the planet gets greener by the second, wine retailers are busy making room for a new category. That category is "carbon neutral", and it'll be coming soon to a wine aisle near you. While the rise of carbon neutral products has been inevitable given the poor health of our planet, you'll appreciate that for a winery to be 100 per cent carbon neutral – given that carbon dioxide is the by-product of fermentation – has up until recently, been very difficult indeed. With the help of carbon traders, those emissions that cannot be controlled can now be offset – a process that involves the winery being charged for the amount of trees that will need to be replanted in order to draw the same amount of carbon from the air. New Zealand's Grove Mill were the first and were quickly joined by the likes of Western Australia's Cullen, the Barossa Valley's Elderton, and South Africa's Backsburg,

Currently, the wine industry is looking at all number of ways it can save on energy and reduce the size of its carbon footprint. At ground level there is an increase in the number of energy efficient wineries, drawing on both solar and wind power, and many now include waste-water treatment plants. There are plans afoot to ship far more wine in bulk with a view to bottling closer to the point of sale, thus reducing the amount of energy used during the shipping process. Another initiative will see lighter glass and the introduction of PET plastic bottles which, all told, could reduce emissions by as much as 35 per cent. Many producers are already recycling as much as 80 per cent of their packaging.

Two Hands Brilliant Disguise Moscato 2008
Barossa Valley
Australia

Lemon, strawberry, pistachio, blood orange, fennel, mint – no matter what your favourite flavour of *gelati* may be, if you're after a foolproof dessert and wine combination, this is it. Light, sweet, and a little bit fizzy, the weight and sweetness of Moscato mirrors the weight and sweetness of *gelati* beautifully, while the bubbles in the wine work to clean and refresh your palate. As it involves little more than scooping *gelati* into a bowl and pulling the cork from a bottle, you have zero excuses for not having a go. This is a lovable addition to the Two Hands portfolio that already contains some of the Barossa's best wines.

get it from...

£8.99

Philglas & Swiggot
Noel Young Wines
Ann et Vin
Alliance Wines

Quinta de la Rosa Aguia 2006
Douro
Portugal

These are exciting times for Portugal –
particularly in the dry red table wine
department – and the Bergqvist
family's Quinta de la Rosa is certainly
one estate worth keeping an eye on.
Since 1992, winemaking has been
overseen by Jorge Moreira, and from
much-loved favourites such as Vale de
Clara right the way to Aguia, the latest
red offering, quality has improved out
of sight. A blend of Touriga Nacional,
Tinta Barocca, and Touriga Franca, this
is a deeply coloured and concentrated
wine with masses of dark dried fruit,
smoke, and spice on the nose. In the
mouth prepare yourself for "inky" and
"full", while bright acidity, cedary oak,
and some fine grippy tannins complete
the picture.

get it from...

£12.80

Selfridges & Co
Green & Blue
Wine in Cornwall
Fields, Morris
 & Verdin

Sainsbury's "Taste the Difference" Gewurztraminer 2006
Alsace
France

To make the classic Thai salad *som tam* – smash two cloves of garlic together with two small chilis, a few green beans, and a couple of small ripe tomatoes. Add lime juice, fish sauce, and palm sugar to taste, then two handfuls of shredded papaya and half a handful of peanuts – and there you have it. This wine is curvaceous, dry Alsatian Gewurztraminer charged with an exotic range of aromas including lychee, jasmine, and musk. This is followed closely by a beautifully structured mouthful of wine that is both oily in texture and low in acidity making it an ideal match with full-flavoured spicy dishes such as *som tam*.

And by that I don't mean burying your head in a stack of wine books (though it's worth having a few). Just go out and find yourself a good food and wine magazine, a decent wine website, or the regular wine column in your favourite paper and read. Every writer has a different style just as they have different tastes in wine. Find out what works for you.

Do a bit of reading...

Salomon Undhof Riesling 2007
Kremstal
Austria

The cool of the Kremstal region, west of Vienna, is home to more than its fair share of seafood-friendly, dry white wines – which is great should you happen to find yourself with the particularly Riesling-friendly combination of watermelon, fresh picked crab, mint, coriander, lime juice, and palm sugar. From Salomon – one of the region's star estates – this is light, dry, and bracing Riesling with terrific sour-citrus fruit intensity. Wrapped around a core of fresh lime, expect to find aromas of miso, lanolin, and apricot, while in your mouth it comes across as citrus-tipped and direct, with focused acidity, and great length of flavour.

get it from...

£11.95

Lea and Sandeman

get it from...

£8.99–9.99

Waitrose (labelled as "Santorini Assyrtiko")
The Wine Society
Tanners Wine
  Merchants
Adnams Wines
Fortnum & Mason
Halifax Wine
  Company
Eclectic Wines

Hatzidakis Santorini Assyrtiko 2007
Santorini
Greece

Char-grilled pork skewers, a squeeze of lemon, a dollop of good Greek yoghurt, and a little salad of tomato, cucumber, capers, and dill will be all you'll need to stand up to this great dry white from the volcanic island of Santorini. Haridimos Hatzidakis is widely acknowledged for his strict viticultural practices – which, in this case, draw on closely planted, old vine fruit. Bright yellow/green to look at, the nose shows grapefruit citrus, marinated pepper, and zero oak influence. The palate is tight, clean, and dry, with stunning intensity of ripe stone fruit.

Although wine today is a very different beast to wine 20 years ago, not every bottle of wine on the shelf is designed to drink well within seconds of you leaving the supermarket. Some bottles will need time to gather dust before really showing their best, and getting hold of them shouldn't cost you a fortune, or even require you to own a fancy cellar. Wine is an amazing drink, and some of it is made all the more amazing by time. So, go on, make patience your virtue this year, as these are the 20 wines well worth waiting for.

20 wines to blow the rent on

splurge

Billecart-Salmon Brut Rosé NV

Champagne
France

If love is in the air in your neck of the woods, then this cracking rosé from one of Champagne's much-loved stars is an essential splurge. Assembled from 40 per cent Chardonnay, 20 per cent Pinot Meunier, and 40 per cent Pinot Noir – eight per cent of which is made into a still red wine and then back blended into the finished product – "Billy" rosé is little short of love in a glass. From its salmon pink tone and delicate nose of ripe Pinot fruit, summer flowers, and spice through to its pure and tightly structured palate, this wine consistently rates as my favourite rosé Champagne and is chock full of style and grace.

get it from...

£42.00

Oddbins
Berry Bros & Rudd
Lay & Wheeler
Lea and Sandeman
Philglas & Swiggot
Selfridges & Co
Harvey Nichols
Jenners
Billecart-Salmon
   UK

Egly-Ouriet
Blanc de Noirs NV
Champagne
France

get it from...

£59.95

Lea and Sandeman

The Egly family are something of an anomaly in Champagne. For starters they are a small family-owned and run operation. They also happen to own many of their own vineyards, giving them greater control over their fruit source. To that end the Eglys also buck the trend of using any kind of chemical herbicides, pesticides, or fungicides by choosing to employ the skills of Claude Bourguignon – one of the world's foremost soil experts. Drawn from vineyards ranging from 30 to 50 years of age, and bottled with zero *dosage* (a sweetened base wine), expect a rich, leesy nose crammed with intense Pinot fruit and spice. The palate is precise, dry, beautifully structured, and built for special occasions.

Reality bites

Boot Camp, *Wife Swap*, *Big Brother* – I've got a reality TV idea for you. It's called "Pick a Winner", and, while the title needs work, it involves taking anyone who thinks tasting wine for a living sounds easy and subjecting them to a week in the life of a wine judge – their aim to pick the best wines from thousands.

Day one will see our contestants taste and write notes on 100 or so wines in the morning, then struggle through a further 100 after lunch. We'll be amazed as they finish the day with a couple of cold beers, we'll cringe as they chat and forget their teeth are stained purple, laugh when they fall asleep on the train, and cry as they have to get up and do it all again the next morning. For many seasoned campaigners of the International Wine Show circuit, this is all in a day's work.

While wine judging may well be a skill in itself, you should be aware that not all wine shows are held in equal regard, and as consumers, you need to be really careful when blindly buying bottles of wine plastered with gold stickers for this very reason. If you don't know a huge amount about wine, then it's very easy to be lead by aesthetics. A pretty label is a great way to sell an ordinary bottle of wine, while back labels will never tell you "how bad a wine is". It's really important to remember that the reputation of the producer whose name appears on the label counts for everything.

Cims de Porrera Solanes Priorat 2004
Priorat
Spain

The Cims de Porrera ("summits of Porrera") vineyards are located at 400–600m (1,310–1,970ft) above sea level in the rocky hills of the Priorat DO, southwest of Barcelona. This is no country for tractors, and so all harvesting of grapes is done by hand – a level of detail that extends right through to the winery. In the bottle, Solanes is a power-packed and inky mix of old-vine Cariñena – mostly above 60 years of age – Garnacha, Cabernet Sauvignon, and Syrah with real weight and intensity. Expect to find plenty of dark, sun-drenched fruit and spice on the nose, while a mouthful will reveal a lush, inky wave of ripe fruit that's beautifully supported by spicy new oak and a wash of dry, grippy tannins.

Viñedos Orgánicos Emiliana Coyam 2006

Colchagua
Chile

Alvaro Espinoza is not your average Chilean winemaker. Having all but single-handedly pioneered organic and environmentally responsible viticulture in South America during the mid-nineties, Espinoza has now trained his sights on converting all of his 240 hectares (593 acres) of vineyards (spread across Colchagua, Maipo, and Casablanca) to biodynamics. One of the resulting wines, "Coyam" is a lush, expressive mix of low-yielding Cabernet Sauvignon, Merlot, Carmenère, Syrah, and Mourvèdre. It spends near enough 12 months in French oak and is bottled without fining or filtration. This is terrific wine: polished and pure, with a serious core of dark fruit, chocolate, leather, and spice. The palate is sweet, dense, and inky, with fresh acidity and fine, drying tannin.

get it from...

£14.99

The Wine Society
Vintage Roots
Tanners Wine Merchants
Virgin Wines

Escarpment "Kupe" Pinot Noir 2006

Martinborough
New Zealand

Larry McKenna's quest to produce top-drawer Pinot Noir from his Escarpment project has been duly rewarded with the third release of "Kupe" – a snapshot of the close-planted Te Muna Road vineyard in Martinborough. Concentrated, perfumed, and with more than a glancing nod towards Burgundy, the '06 model displays a tightly wound core of dark, sweet fruit underpinned by hints of earth, spice, and deftly handled cedary oak – 50 per cent of which is new. Weighing in at 14.1 per cent ABV, the palate is generous, silky, and long and is testament to McKenna's skill with this difficult child of grape varieties.

Craiglee Shiraz 2005
Sunbury
Australia

Craiglee is a leisurely two-café-lattes' drive northwest of Melbourne. As one of Victoria's first vineyards, today, under current owner Pat Carmody, it remains a benchmark within the Australian wine community. Included in the coveted Langton's *Classification of Australian Wine* and a regular darling of the wine press, Craiglee's spicy, cool-climate Shiraz is simply one of the finest examples of its kind produced in the Southern Hemisphere. 2005 was a textbook vintage, and the wines have Craiglee's typical nose of blood plum, liqueur cherry, and ground black pepper. The palate is spicy and seamless with a firm and balanced structure that ensures this wine has a long future.

Niepoort
Redoma Tinto 2005
Douro
Portugal

First released in 1991, "Redoma Tinto" was Douro-maverick Dirk Niepoort's first foray into Portuguese table wine. Carved from an indigenous mix of Tinta Amarela, Tinta Roriz, and Touriga Franca, and from vines that average 60 years of age, expect a nose stacked with cool, dark fruit, Coca Cola, smoke, cedar, and spice. The palate is plush and inky with plenty of sweet, liquorice-like fruit, decent grip, and good balance. Acidity is bright and oak is French, while the overall balance is beautiful.

Bouchard Père & Fils Volnay "Clos des Chênes" 2005

Burgundy
France

2005 was a dreamy vintage in Burgundy. For starters, a mild, sunny growing season ensured that what was hanging on the vine at harvest time was top drawer. The resulting wines are stunners. From the teeny tiny chalk/clay-based "Clos des Chênes" vineyard – which at 0.85 hectares (2.1 acres) produces little more than 4,000 bottles per year – expect to meet a wave of ripe raspberry and cherry Pinot fruit, while in the mouth there is huge intensity, velvet-like texture, and fine structure. There is real depth and richness here, but not at the expense of the acidity and grip that defines this vintage's top wines. Also, when it comes to doing your shopping, just be sure you're buying the right Bouchard, as there are others!

get it from...

£35.00–40.99

Majestic Wine Warehouse
Fine & Rare Wines
J E Fells

Aldo Conterno Barolo "Bussia Soprana" 2004
Piedmont
Italy

As one of Italy's most highly respected producers, wines from Aldo Conterno's Piedmont estate rarely, if ever, leave you feeling disappointed, or – given Barolo's soaring prices – short-changed. With two feet in Barolo's traditional camp, these wines display an incredible hand-made feel, yet manage to retain charm and class by the bagful. Sourced from vineyards around Bussia (not including the *crus* of Romirasco, Cicala, or Colonnello), the entry-level "Bussia Soprana" bears all the hallmarks of Conterno's magic touch. On board you'll find a core of morello cherry, rose petal, black olive, rosemary, tobacco, and exotic spice. The palate is delicately textured, yet at the same time, intensely fruited – the absolute benchmark introduction to Barolo.

get it from...

£56.95

Fortnum & Mason
Harvey Nichols
Nickolls & Perks
Philglas & Swiggot
Liberty Wines

Paul Jaboulet Aîné
Hermitage La Chapelle 2005
Northern Rhône
France

Sold to the Frey family (owners of Château La Lagune in Bordeaux) in 2005, there has been a real return to form at Jaboulet in recent times. With styles produced both north and south of Lyon, the undoubted jewel in the Jaboulet crown is the prestigious La Chapelle from Hermitage in the North. One-hundred per cent Syrah and a blend of selected plots from within the La Chapelle vineyard, expect a deep and pure wine sporting a nose of bright cherry, plum, forest fruit, meat, smoke, and spice. There is excellent weight in the mouth, too, with nicely knit oak – none of which is new – followed closely by bright acidity and a wash of firm grainy tannin.

get it from...

£113.95

Farr Vintners
WoodWinters Wines & Whiskies
The Secret Cellar
Liberty Wines

Marcarini Barolo La Serra 2003
Piedmont
Italy

From Marcarini's 3.5-hectare (8.6-acre) "La Serra" vineyard perched high up in the hills of La Morra, this is a very traditional style of Barolo that speaks volumes about where it's from, rather than how it's made. Vineyards are composted organically and traditional methods of farming are employed where possible. More elegant than its muscular stable mate "Brunate", expect to find an extraordinary nose of rose, tar, black olive, rosemary, rolling tobacco, and dry woody herbs. The palate is delicate, linear, and beautifully textured with very pure fruit and a wash of dry, grainy tannins. Ample acidity should keep things in check for many moons to come.

Isole e Olena
Cepparello 2003
Tuscany
Italy

WINE OF THE YEAR

After the disappointingly wet 2002, the abnormally hot 2003 brought about further frustrations to many Italian growers – particularly those in Tuscany. From a year that produced a raft of over-ripe and unbalanced wines, Paolo de Marchi's flagship wine, Cepparello, is both an exception and a serious show-stopper. Assembled from 100 per cent Sangiovese, this multi-layered wine packs a dense core of dark morello cherry fruit surrounded by aromas of fresh tobacco, liquorice, leather, dried spice, and deftly used French oak – one third of which is new. For such a warm vintage there is real elegance on the palate, too, with a bright mineral texture and a terrific intensity of fruit. It winds up with a wash of mouth-coating, yet fine Sangiovese tannin.

get it from...

£37.95

Noel Young Wines
Philglas & Swiggot
Valvona & Crolla
Bennetts Fine
   Wines
The Sampler
Liberty Wines

Eben Sadie
Sequillo Red 2004
Franschhoek
South Africa

A straight-talking, no-nonsense Rhône-style blend of Syrah, Mourvèdre, and Grenache, "Sequillo" is intelligent everyday drinking red from one of South Africa's most exciting young winemakers, Eben Sadie. Having travelled and worked extensively throughout Europe, Sadie returned to South Africa with a desire to produce wines with real spirit and a sense of place. Efforts are concentrated in the vineyards, while in the winery everything is either done by hand or gravity. Sitting underneath the more serious "Columella" and "Palladius", "Sequillo" is a gluggable medium-bodied wine loaded with bright raspberry and sour cherry fruit, trademark Rhône pepper, and zero oak influence – an absolutely delicious wine.

get it from...

£13.00–15.00

Berry Bros & Rudd
Sommelier Wine Co
Villeneuve Wines
Richards Walford

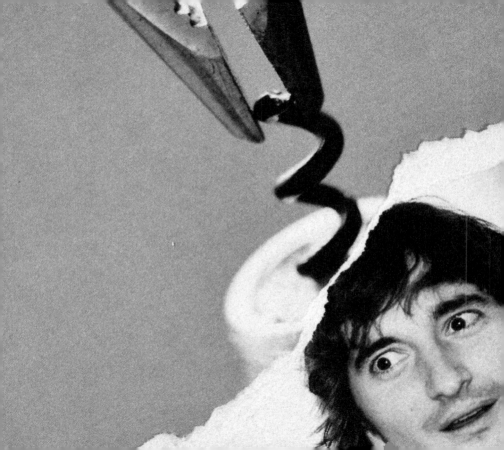

Gaia
Assyrtiko Thalassitis 2007
Santorini
Greece

One half of Gaia estate, Yiannis
Paraskevopoulos, is a leading light in
Greece's small but flourishing wine
scene. Also a lecturer in oenology,
Paraskevopoulos has played a big
role in shaping the development of
Greece's winemaking future. Having
built Gaia's reputation for producing
pristine and mineral examples of white
variety Assyrtiko (as-SEAR-tick-oh)
from Santorini's poor black volcanic
soil during the mid-nineties, this
remains a serious passion. Thalassitis
is taken from 70–80 year-old low-
yielding, un-grafted Assyrtiko vines.
Fermentation in stainless steel is long
and cool, giving clean, mineral, softly
honeyed, and bright citrus-fruit
character to the end wine. In the
mouth it's both firm and dry, with
real intensity of citrus fruit and crisp
acidity that keeps things running in
a straight line.

Giaconda Nantua
Les Deux 2007
Beechworth (Victoria)
Australia

Giaconda is now something
of a legend. Not only does Rick
Kinzbrunner's Chardonnay rank among
the world's best, but it is arguably
Australia's finest. In 2001, Kinzbrunner
added two new lines to his portfolio:
"Aeolia", a 100 per cent Roussanne
given the same Rolls Royce treatment
as his prized Chardonnay, and
"Nantua Les Deux", a delicious
blend of Chardonnay and Roussanne
that offers serious value for money.
Grapefruit and nectarine-like fruit take
centre stage alongside aromas of fresh
toast, grilled hazelnut, and pork rind.
The palate is long, rich, minerally, and
lush. A worthy and welcome addition
to the Giaconda stable.

Water into wine

You know that we're talking about a precious commodity when at up to £1 (AUS$2) a bottle, a single litre of water is often more expensive than a single litre of petrol.

Water is one of the most important ingredients in wine production. Without water, you simply cannot make wine. The irony is that while the wine industry stands to feel the effects of climate change long before most, it also happens to be one of agriculture's biggest water users.

To give you an idea just how big that is, to make a single litre of wine in Australia takes near enough to seven litres of water. And that's just to make the wine. To grow the grapes that eventually make that single litre of wine takes closer to 400 litres of water. In case you are still reeling from that figure – that was around 400 litres of water on average just to make a single litre of wine. As a result, water-saving initiatives are fast becoming both mandatory and commonplace within the Australian wine industry.

Many of Australia's biggest wine producers have already developed and installed their own waste-water treatment plants allowing them to re-use reclaimed water from their wineries to irrigate their vineyards. Other initiatives include the use of various mulches in the vineyards in order to minimize the amount of evaporation from the soil, and employing the use of soil monitors to regulate irrigation throughout the vineyards, irrigating only when needed and only at night in order to reduce evaporation.

It might not sound like much, but it's a start.

Pierre Morey
Meursault 2005
Burgundy
France

As winemaker for the iconic Domaine Leflaive since 1995, Pierre Morey knows a thing or two about producing complex, multi-tiered, and age-worthy examples of Chardonnay. As at Domaine Leflaive, biodynamic practices (employed since 1997) play a huge role in Morey's own vineyards – 9 hectares (22.2 acres) in total, spread across holdings in Meursault, Monthélie, Pommard, and Puligny-Montrachet. From a brilliant year for white wine in Burgundy, this is stylish, full-flavoured Chardonnay crammed with aromas of grapefruit, nectarine, hazelnut, and sweet spice. The palate is pure, mineral, racy, and wound-up tightly with plenty to offer underneath. In a word, awesome!

get it from...

£37.31

Justerini & Brooks

£10.49–11.49

Halewood International
Chalié, Richards
& Co

Highbank Coonawarra 2003
Coonawarra
Australia

Dennis Vice has long championed the benefits of organic viticulture, and this wine – with considerable age already under it's belt – comes from the tiny, organic, Vice family vineyard on Coonawarra's famed terra rossa soil. Basket-pressing and a decent stint in fine-grained French oak has produced a nose with a confit of dark fruit, leather, and cedar, while the palate is lush and seamless with real weight and intensity. That power is matched beautifully by soft acidity and a wave of firm, drying tannin. Stick it away for a while or decant and enjoy now.

Planeta Cometa 2007
Sicily
Italy

As the wines of southern Italy continue to win hearts the world over, Sicily's star producer, Planeta, remains the measuring stick for quality and success. This is the estate that, through serious attention in the vineyard and a real focus on both international and indigenous varieties, has really helped to put Sicily on the wine map. The latest offering of the flagship white, Cometa, is a mighty example of Fiano di Avellino (one of Campania's five appellations), which bears considerable elegance and restraint for a wine of its size. Expect grapefruit, white peach, and fennel on the nose, while in your mouth it's rich, spicy, and structured beautifully with gentle acidity and flavour that seems to hang around forever.

get it from...

£25.00

Majestic Wine Warehouse
Enotria Winecellars

Zind Humbrecht Riesling Herrenweg de Turkheim 2005
Alsace
France

Olivier Humbrecht carves out some of the most insanely pure, rich, and expressive wines to be found anywhere in Alsace. Serious attention to detail in the vineyard – incorporating high density planting, super-low yields, and biodynamics – bears wines that simply ooze varietal expression without compromising on terroir. This is textbook Riesling from the deep and gravelly Herrenweg vineyard south of Turkheim, where aromas of grapefruit, lime, and minerals make way for a focused, steely mouthful of wine that's balanced beautifully by trademark acidity and terrific length of flavour.

Au Bon Climat Wild Boy Chardonnay 2007
California
USA

Putting the tie-dyed, Purple Haze-like label to one side for a moment, Jim Clendenen is a master when it comes to creating complex, nutty, citrus-laden examples of Chardonnay that burst with personality and style. From tightly packed and intense grapefruit character through to aromas of cashew and hazelnut, this is a lesson in just how good New World Chardonnay can be. Better still, it tastes every inch as good as it smells, with focused citrus fruit, great length of flavour, and screw-capped freshness.

get it from...

£14.00

Berry Bros & Rudd
Harvey Nichols
Fields, Morris & Verdin

Find a decent wine shop and get to know the guys behind the counter. Tell them what type of wine you like drinking and get them to offer some recommendations. The more specific you can be about what you do or don't like, the better your chances are of ending up with a decent bottle. And, most importantly, try as many different wines as you can.

Make some new friends

Although wine today is a very different beast to wine 20 years ago, not every bottle of wine on the shelf is designed to drink well within seconds of you leaving the supermarket. Some bottles will need time to gather dust before really showing their best and getting hold of them shouldn't cost you a fortune, or even require you to own a fancy cellar. Wine is an amazing drink, and some of it is made all the more amazing by time. So, go on, make patience your virtue this year, as these are the 20 wines well worth waiting for.

20 wines for drinking later

stash

Pol Roger Brut Réserve NV
Champagne
France

While most non-vintage Champagnes or sparkling wines are designed to maintain a consistent house style with early consumption in mind, those of you with enough patience to wait a couple of years will be duly rewarded – particularly in the case of the much-loved Pol Roger Brut Réserve. This is a real essay in style and value, with equal parts Chardonnay, Pinot Noir, and Pinot Meunier, and assembled from around 60 base wines. Expect aromas and flavours of fresh bread, marzipan, and citrus marmalade, while in the mouth it is long, fine, and packed with elegance and finesse.

Fonseca Vintage Port 2003
Douro
Portugal

Designed to make you wait, vintage port does its ageing in bottle and often needs a couple of decades (seriously) to unwind. With time, these wines reveal a deep and complex nose of dark spiced fruits, bitter chocolate, and nicely worn leather. What often starts out tasting harsh and extractive in its youth, usually blossoms into a plush, bittersweet, and delicious mouthful of wine with age. Fonseca has produced many of the region's finest ports since the eighteenth century, and continues today as the measuring stick of quality for many others. Hold until 2020 – if you can bear it!

get it from...

£65

Lea and Sandeman
Berry Bros & Rudd
Farr Vintners
Bibendum Wine
Mentzendorff

Palacios Remondo
La Montesa 2005
Rioja
Spain

get it from...

£12.50

Berry Bros & Rudd
Fields, Morris & Verdin

Priorat's vinous superstar, Alvaro Palacios, produces some of the most sought-after – not to mention frighteningly expensive – wines in Spain. Thankfully, his family's estate in nearby Rioja offers wines that are a little easier on the wallet. They are also exceptionally good quality, built to go the distance, and should easily drink well over the next 15 years. This wine – from old-vine Tempranillo – is a perfect example. Find masses of dark, sun-drenched fruit and spice flooding your nose, while a mouthful will reveal a lush inky wave of ripe dark fruit, spicy new oak, and a wash of dry grippy tannins.

Abadia Retuerta
Selección Especial 2005
Castilla y León
Spain

Even if it doesn't quite fall into the bounds of the Ribera del Duero DO, Abadia Retuerta (in Sardon de Duero) – which in 1988 received a much needed injection of capital, courtesy of pharmaceutical giant Novartis – produces some incredibly classy wines that comfortably compete with many of nearby Ribera's more expensive examples. From a polished blend of Tempranillo, Cabernet, and Merlot, Selección Especial is a clean, modern, and deliciously drinkable wine with a nose of pure black cherry, raspberry, tobacco leaf, and spice. The palate is medium-bodied and firmly structured with plenty of dark berry fruit and firm, chewy tannins. Stick it away for the next decade.

get it from...

£15.95

Halifax Wine Company
Reserve Wines
Whole Foods
  Market
The Flying
  Corkscrew
Bentley's
Liberty Wines

Wakefield St Andrews Cabernet Sauvignon 2004
Clare Valley
Australia

Wakefield (known as Taylors in Australia) consistently turns out one of the country's top examples of Cabernet Sauvignon. From one of the better Clare vintages in recent memory, St Andrews 2004 is a sleek and stylish wine that is destined to be long lived. Sealed with a shiny blue screw cap, expect a nose of blackcurrant, sweet plum, and aniseed, while in your mouth it's long, sleek, and spicy with sparingly used oak. Fermentation was long and cool. The oak was French and in contact with the wine for 12–14 months. Drink it closer to 2015 than 2010.

Partridges
Swig

Vergelegen Mill Race Cabernet / Merlot 2005
Stellenbosch
South Africa

The larger-than-life André van Rensburg is responsible for producing a number of the Cape's finest reds, and his Mill Race Cabernet/Merlot is certainly no exception. Bringing together top-drawer New World fruit and classic European styling, this is an elegant blend that, while drinking beautifully now, will definitely benefit from a short stint in the cellar. From selected vineyards, this is a terrific starting point for those who like their reds richly fruited and ready to drink. On closer inspection you'll find a solid core of sweet black fruit, while in your mouth it's focused and plush, with well-rounded tannins and a long dry finish.

Ca'Viola Dolcetto Bric du Luv 2004
Piedmont
Italy

As one of Piedmont's "Nuevo Radici" (New Radicals), Beppe Ca'Viola produces a densely fruited, modern style of Dolcetto that, to look at, is nearer jet-black than purple. Expect to find a compact nose of damson berry, black fruits, and leather, while in the mouth it's full and dry with pure dark fruit, fresh acidity, and balanced nicely by a wall of dry chunky tannin. This is heavy artillery that should be kept in the cellar for the better part of the next decade.

get it from...

£22.00

Field & Fawcett Wine Merchants & Delicatessen
Grape-Juice
Noel Young Wines
Caviste
New Generation Wines

Quartz Reef
Pinot Noir 2007
Central Otago
New Zealand

Over time, Martinborough has set the pace for New Zealand Pinot Noir, but a rise in the number of staggeringly good wines from Central Otago (and, more recently, Marlborough) has really put a cat among the pigeons. And, while Central Otago might not have vine age on its side, it does have a dreamy mix of clones together with unique microclimates perfectly suited to producing great Pinot Noir. Rudi Bauer's Quartz Reef ranks among the region's finest. To see it at its best, hold on until 2010.

get it from...

£15.99

Majestic Wine Warehouse
Wheeler Cellars
Lay & Wheeler

Livered

All my mates are detoxing. "Need to give our livers a chance to do what they're made for," says one. Whatever. Given that I taste wine for a living, the concept of detox isn't one that sits all that comfortably with me. I momentarily think about going in to bat for wine and its many health benefits, before realizing that in the case of more than just a few of my mates, wine probably isn't the main offender. There are very few days in my life when I do not drink. It's my job, and besides, I enjoy a couple of glasses of wine with my dinner. Although in saying that, rarely do I drink more than that during the week, and if I do get drunk, it's never on wine.

There was a time not so long ago when wine was seen as the medical world's great hope. The combination of alcohol and acidity proved to be a winning combination in tackling all manner of injury and illness and its healing properties were praised and prescribed by doctors right around the globe. But with the latter part of the twentieth century came advances in medicine and technology, not to mention different ways of thinking. For the first time the healing properties of wine were scrutinized and Prohibition in the US censored any mention of alcohol, wine included.

Today, with modern thinking, further medical advances, and interest in subjects such as the French Paradox, most experts would argue that the majority of healthy people who drink wine regularly and in moderation remain healthy.

Bottoms up!

£22.95

Averys Wine Merchants
Berry Bros & Rudd
Goedhuis & Company
Direct Wines
Folly Wines

Nicolas Potel Volnay 2006
Burgundy
France

Sandwiched between Pommard and Meursault, Volnay-based négociant Nicolas Potel produces a range of ecologically sound wines from a number of vineyards throughout Burgundy. With close to 40 per cent of this blend sourced from *premier cru* vineyards, and much of it from old vines, expect a nose rich with typical and pronounced Pinot Noir character. Perhaps the best range of Potel wines to date, these are, at best, multi-layered, purely fruited, slightly animal, textured, seductive, slinky, fine, and most of all, magic. If you stash them, they'll only get better.

William Fèvre
Petit Chablis 2006
Burgundy
France

Classically styled and beautifully made, this is pristine Chablis from one of the region's brightest stars. As some of the most pure expressions of Chardonnay you can find, wines from the Fèvre stable tend towards being squeaky clean, mineral in texture, and often void of oak influence. Aromas and flavours range from lemon and honey through hay to chalk. Taken from the Chablis sub-district of Petit Chablis, this fine example from the highly regarded 2006 vintage is certainly no exception. Stick some away for the better part of the next decade.

Kooyong Estate Chardonnay 2006
Mornington Peninsula
Australia

Having built a solid reputation as a producer of top shelf Pinot Noir, Kooyong winemaker Sandro Mosele has turned his attention to Chardonnay. All bases are covered: from the cheap and cheerful "Massale" through to the far more serious single vineyard examples. Of the range the "Estate" label Chardonnay effortlessly knits New World richness to Old World structure and charm. On the nose expect to unearth all kinds of amazing stuff such as crème brûlée, cashew, grapefruit, nectarine, and pork rind, while in your mouth it's rich and intense with minerally texture and jaw-dropping intensity of flavour. Hold until 2015.

get it from...

£18.35

Great Western Wine
Harvey Nichols
Swig

Pierre Morey
Bourgogne Blanc 2005
Burgundy
France

Pierre Morey is currently responsible for producing some of the greatest examples of Chardonnay on the planet – complex, stylish examples that have serious ability to go the distance in the cellar. And while this is maybe Morey's most basic example of the variety, it is certainly no slouch, and worth every penny. Green-gold to look at, expect to find a tight and perfumed nose of grapefruit, nectarine, hazelnut, and sweet spice. The palate shows extraordinary intensity of fruit, bright mineral-texture, and flavour that goes on and on and on. Watch it unwind over the coming decade.

Pieropan
Soave Classico 2007
Veneto
Italy

Taken from the slopes of Monte Foscarino, northeast of Verona, Pieropan Soave Classico is stunning wine from one of Soave's finest producers. This is also a wine that over the coming 10–15 years will develop beautifully in the bottle, taking on aromas and flavours of bright citrus marmalade, quince, and honey. But, if you're not the kind of person who likes to wait, then open one now and expect a nose that's rich with aromas of lemon, beeswax, and marzipan, while in your mouth, rounded citrus fruit bound by lovely mineral texture is the key.

get it from...

£10.95

Harrods
Averys Wine Merchants
Luvians Bottleshop
Villeneuve Wines
WoodWinters Wines & Whiskies
Wimbledon Wine Cellar
Highbury Vintners
Bacchus Wine
Liberty Wines

Louis Latour Marsannay 2006
Burgundy
France

Wine producers since the seventeenth century, Louis Latour are one of the oldest and most respected négociant houses in Burgundy today. Producing a raft of wines from within the boundaries of the Côte d'Or, this robust and utterly drinkable example of Pinot Noir from Marsannay in the extreme north is a cracker. Oozing varietal character and charm, here you'll find generous cherry and raspberry fruit, smells of game and sweet spice, silky mouth-feel, chewy tannins characteristic of the region, and superb length of flavour.

Tahbilk Marsanne 2006
Nagambie Lakes (Victoria)
Australia

Sporting a string of accolades that would make most competitors blush, Tahbilk Marsanne is one quiet achieving Aussie wine that consistently overdelivers considering its price tag. With fruit harvested from plantings dating back to 1927, here's a wine that – while drinking beautifully right this second – will hit its teens developing into a complex and honeyed wine. Packing green apple, pear, honeysuckle, and plenty of citrus zip and zing, the welcome addition of a screwcap since the release of the 2005 vintage is great news and should see these already long-lived wines long outlive most of us!

get it from...

£9.99

Thresher
Ehrmanns

Pyramid Valley Lebecca Vineyard Riesling 2005
Canterbury
New Zealand

get it from...

£14.50

Swig

Mouthwatering wine from one of the most exciting producers in New Zealand. Mike Weersing studied winemaking in Burgundy, and has also worked for some of the planet's finest producers. In his Canterbury-based Pyramid Valley vineyards he incorporates biodynamic principles wherever possible to produce wines like this knockout Germanic-styled Lebecca Riesling. Sweetness, acidity, and alcohol are perfectly tuned to give a terrific proposition for your cellar. Expect aromas of pretty jasmine flowers, mandarin, and Golden Delicious apples that make way for a delicate mouthful of wine that's off-dry and balanced beautifully by mineral texture and super fresh acidity.

Leasingham Bin 7 Clare Valley Riesling 2007

Clare Valley
Australia

Having set up operations in 1893, Leasingham planted its first Riesling vines during the early part of the forties. Knockout examples have been produced from this estate ever since. Bin 7 is made up of fruit sourced from a combination of vineyards from various pockets in South Australia's Riesling capital, the Clare Valley. Straw green in colour, this is classically-styled Clare Riesling, from its nose of spring flowers and Kaffir lime to its rich and steely palate. And, while this is a mouthwatering drink right now, five years in the cellar – ten if you're really disciplined – will see Bin 7 blossom beautifully into middle age.

get it from...

£9.99

Bibendum
Matthew Clark
The Revelstoke Wine Co
Wine Studio
Constellation

Dönnhoff Oberhauser Leistenberg Riesling Kabinett 2007
Nahe
Germany

The decomposed grey slate and volcanic rock of Oberhauser's best vineyards provide the ultimate starting point for one of Germany's top producers. Dönnhoff has been making wine in the Nahe since 1750 and these are wines with terrific richness, purity, and balance – all characteristic of the region's top examples. Tightly sprung with amazing depth and purity, both the nose and palate show intense citrus and tropical fruits, power, and youth. There is stunning balance between sweetness and acidity. Drinking beautifully now, but with us for the long haul.

get it from...

£14.49–15.49

Noel Young Wines
David Roberts Domaines
Connolly's
Hicks & Don
ABS Wine Agencies

I know it's not PC to admit so, but I love flying. Yes, I'm acutely aware of my responsibilities and as a result ride my bike whenever possible, catch the train when it's not, drive if I have to, and fly only when it's absolutely necessary. But it's not always that simple, and working for an organisation with venues either side of the equator, flying has become an integral part of my job. Call me strange, but the idea of sailing backward and forward from the UK to Australia three times a year doesn't exactly fill me with enthusiasm.

But, much as I enjoy climbing aboard a Jumbo, the effect of altitude on our senses is dramatic. Two things cause this. The first is the relatively low humidity of the cabin, that in turn affects our ability to smell, while low cabin pressure acts like anaesthetic on our taste-buds. As a result many wines will seem less fruity, more acidic, and higher in tannin than they appear on the ground. With this in mind, most airlines employ a crack team of experts who regularly sniff, swirl, and slurp their way through hundreds of wines in order to dig out the wines that perform best in the air.

Cooking is a brilliant way to learn more about wine. Getting your head around different smells, flavours, and textures in food will undoubtedly help you better understand what's going on in a glass of wine – not to mention giving you a major head start when it comes to pairing wine and food.

Get busy in the kitchen

McWilliams Mount Pleasant Elizabeth Semillon 2007
Hunter Valley
Australia

Hunter Semillon is one of the most iconic wine styles produced in Australia. The best examples display an effortless ability to age – often outliving those that put them together. Hot off the press, Elizabeth 2007 is a pup and, provided you look after it, should comfortably cruise well into middle age. Currently you can expect to find a tightly wound wine where lemons, tart green apples, and bees wax all make an appearance on the nose. In your mouth, the palate is similarly tight and firm. Given time – and we're talking 10–15 years – this wine will unwind to reveal a richly fruited core of citrus marmalade, honeyed toast, and spice.

get it from...

£9.99

Morrisons
Beaconsfield Wine Cellar
Coe Vintners
Partridges On-line
  Grocery Store
E & J Gallo

Peter Lehmann Margaret Barossa Semillon 2002
Barossa Valley
Australia

get it from...

£11.99

Tesco
Asda
Oddbins
Peter Lehmann
   UK

Named after the great Margaret Lehmann – wife of Peter, the champion of Barossa Semillon – "Margaret" has already gathered quite a collection of accolades in its debut year, including "Wine of the Competition" at the prestigious Sydney International Wine Competition 2008. Released with five years' age, this opens with a classic Semillon nose of ripe citrus fruit, honey, and spice. And expect to find a tight and firmly structured mouthful of wine that has real intensity of flavour, thanks to top shelf, old-vine Barossa fruit, alongside hints of smoke and spice. This is beautifully structured wine that, given the right conditions, will happily live on for the next decade and possibly beyond.

Stockists (UK)

Abbey Wines
01896 823224

ABS (Awin Barratt Siegel)
   Wine Agencies
www.abswineagencies.co.uk
01780 755810

Adnams Wines
www.adnamswines.co.uk
01502 727222

Alliance Wines
www.alliancewine.co.uk
01505 506060

Andrew Chapman Fine Wines
www.surf4wine.co.uk
01235 821539

Ann et Vin
www.annetvin.com
01636 700900

Armit
www.armit.co.uk
020 7908 0600

Asda
www.asda-
   beerwinessspirits.co.uk

Averys Wine Merchants
www.averys.com
0845 8630995

Bacchus Wine
www.bacchus.co.uk
01234 711140

Beaconsfield Wine Cellar
www.beaconsfieldwinecellars.
   com
01494 675545

Bennetts Fine Wine Merchants
www.bennettsfinewines.com
01386 840392

Bentley's (Wine Merchants
   of Ludlow)
www.bentleyswine.com
01584 875520

Berkmann Wine Cellars
www.berkmann.co.uk
020 7609 4711

Berry Bros & Rudd
www.bbr.com
0870 900 4300

Bibendum Wine
www.bibendum-wine.co.uk
020 7722 5577

Billecart-Salmon UK
020 8405 6345

Bon Coeur Fine Wines
www.bcfw.co.uk
020 7622 5244

Booths
www.booths-
   supermarkets.co.uk
01772 693800

The Bottle Stop
0161 4394904

The Bristol Wine Company
www.thebristolwinecompany.
   co.uk
0117 373 0288

The Butlers Wine Cellar
www.butlers-winecellar.co.uk
01273 698 724

Cambridge Wine Merchants
www.cambridgewine.com
01223 568991

Camel Valley
www.camelvalley.com
01208 77959

Caviste
www.caviste.co.uk
01256 770397

C & D Wines
www.canddwines.co.uk
020 8778 1711

Chalié, Richards & Co
www.chalie-richards.co.uk
0845 850 4405

Cheviot Wine Agencies
0141 6499881

Coe Vintners
www.coevintners.co.uk
020 8514 966

Connolly's
www.connollys-wine.co.uk
0121 2369269

Constellation
www.cbrands.eu.com
01483 690000

The Co-operative Group
www.co-operative.coop/food
0800 0686727

David Roberts Domaines
www.davidrobertsdomaines.
   com
01359 271795

D Byrne & Co
www.dbyrne-finewines.co.uk
01200 423152

De Bortoli UK
www.debortoli.com.au
01725 516467

Direct Wines
www.laithwaites.co.uk
0870 066 5689

Divine Fine Wines Ltd
www.divinefinewines.co.uk
0121 4367558 / 07771 978236

Dreyfus, Ashby & Co Ltd
01732 361639

Eclectic Wines
020 7736 3733

Ehrmanns
www.ehrmannswines.co.uk
0207 4181800

E&J Gallo
www.gallo.com

Enotria Winecellars
www.enotria.co.uk
020 8961 5161

Farr Vintners
www.farrvintners.com
020 7821 2000

Field & Fawcett Wine
   Merchants & Delicatessen
www.fieldandfawcett.co.uk
01904 489073

Fields, Morris & Verdin
www.fmvwines.com
020 7921 5300

Fine & Rare Wines
www.frw.co.uk
020 8960 1995

The Fine Wine Company
www.thefinewinecompany.co.uk
0131 6697716

The Flying Corkscrew
www.flyingcorkscrew.co.uk
01442 412311

Folly Wines
www.follywines.co.uk

Fortnum & Mason
www.fortnumandmason.com
020 7734 8040

Gauntleys of Nottingham
www.gauntley-wine.co.uk
0115 9110555

Goedhuis & Company
www.goedhuis.com
020 7793 7900

Grape-Juice
www.grape-juice.com
020 7403 9997

The Great Grog Company
www.greatgrog.co.uk
0131 662 4777

Great Western Wine
www.greatwesternwine.co.uk
01225 322800

The Great Wine Hunter
www.greatwinehunter.co.uk

Green & Blue
www.greenandbluewines.com
020 7498 9648

The Guildford Wine Company
www.theguildfordwine
    company.co.uk
01483 560647

Hailsham Cellars
www.hailshamcellars.com
01323 441212

Halewood International
www.halewood-int.com
01514808800

Halifax Wine Company
www.halifaxwinecompany.com
01422 256333

Handford Wines
www.handford.net
020 7221 9614

Harrods
www.harrods.com
020 7730 1234

Harvey Nichols
www.harveynichols.com
020 7235 5000

H B Clark & Co
www.hbclark.co.uk
01924 373328

Hedley Wright Wine
    Merchants
www.hedleywright.co.uk
01279 465818

Henderson Wines
www.hendersonwines.co.uk
0131 448580

Hicks & Don
www.hicksanddon.co.uk
01380 831234

Highbury Vintners
www.highburyvintners.co.uk
020 7226 1347

Hoults Wine Merchants
www.hoults-
    winemerchants.co.uk
01484 510700

House of Fraser
www.houseoffraser.co.uk

Inverarity Vaults
www.inverarity-vaults.com
01899 308000

J E Fells & Sons
www.fells.co.uk
01442 870900

Jenners (House of Fraser)
www.houseoffraser.co.uk

Justerini & Brooks
www.justerinis.com
020 7484 6400

Lakeland Vintners
www.lakelandvintners.co.uk
01539 821999

Lanson UK
www.lansoninternational.com
020 7499 0070

Lay & Wheeler
www.laywheeler.com
01473 313233

Lea and Sandeman
www.londonfinewine.co.uk
020 7244 0522

Les Vignerons de St Georges
www.les-vignerons.co.uk
01276 850136

Liberty Wines
www.libertywine.co.uk
020 7720 5350

Louis Latour UK
www.louislatour.co.uk
020 7409 7276

Luvians Bottleshop
www.luvians.com
01334 654820

Majestic Wine Warehouse
www.majestic.co.uk
0845 605 6767
(min. purchase: 12 bottles)

Marks & Spencer
www.marksandspencer.com
0845 302 1234

Matthew Clark
www.matthewclark.co.uk
01275 891400

Mentzendorff
www.mentzendorff.co.uk
020 7840 3600

Michael Hall Wines
01932 223398

Mill Hill Wines
www.millhillwines.com
020 8959 6754

Morrisons
www.morrisons.co.uk
0845 611 6111

Negociants UK
www.negociantsuk.com
01582 462859

New Generation Wines
www.newgenerationwines.
    com
020 7403 9997

Nickolls & Perks
www.nickollsandperks.co.uk
01384 394518

Noel Young Wines
www.nywines.co.uk
01223 844744

Novum
www.novumwines.com
020 7820 6720

Oakley Wine Agencies
01787 220070

Oddbins
www.oddbins.com
0800 917 4093

The Oxford Wine Company
www.oxfordwine.co.uk
01865 301144

Oz Wines
www.ozwines.co.uk
0845 450 1261

Partridges On-line
  Grocery Store
www.partridges.co.uk
020 7730 0651

Peter Lehmann Wines UK
www.peterlehmannwines.com
01227 731 353

Philglas & Swiggot
www.philglas-swiggot.co.uk
020 8332 6031

PLB Group Ltd
www.plb.co.uk
01342 318282

Pol Roger UK
www.polroger.co.uk
01432 262800

Private Cellar Ltd
www.privatecellar.co.uk
01353 721999

Raeburn Fine Wines
www.raeburnfinewines.com
0131 3325166

Ravensbourne Wine Co
www.ravensbournewine.co.uk
020 7252 2600

Raymond Reynolds
www.raymondreynolds.co.uk
01663 742230

Reserve Wines
www.reservewines.co.uk
0161 4380101

The Revelstoke Wine Co
www.revelstoke.co.uk
0208 545 0077

Richards Walford
www.r-w.co.uk

Roberson Wine Merchant
www.robersonwinemerchant.
  co.uk
020 7371 2121

R S Wines Ltd
www.rswines.co.uk
01275 331444

Sainsbury's
www.sainsburys.co.uk
0800 636 262

Seckford Wines
www.seckfordwines.co.uk
01394 446622

Selfridges & Co
www.selfridges.com
08708 377 377

Sheridan Cooper's
www.sheridancoopers.co.uk
01273 298117

S H Jones
www.shjoneswines.com
01295 251179

The Sampler
www.thesampler.co.uk
020 7226 9500

The Secret Cellar
www.thesecretcellar.co.uk
01892 537981

Soho Wine Supply
www.sohowine.co.uk
020 7636 8490

Somerfield
www.somerfield.co.uk

Sommelier Wine Co
01481 721677

Stevens Garnier
www.stevensgarnier.co.uk
01865 263300

Stratford's Wine Agencies
www.stratfordwine.co.uk
01628 810606

The Sussex Wine Company
www.thesussexwinecompany.
  co.uk
01323 431143

Swig
www.swig.co.uk
08000 272 272

Tanners Wine Merchants
www.tanners-wines.co.uk
01743 234455

Tesco
www.tesco.com

Thresher
www.victoriawine.co.uk
01707 387200

Valvona & Crolla
www.valvonacrolla.co.uk
0131 5566066

Villeneuve Wines
www.villeneuvewines.com
01721 722500

Vin du Vin
www.vinduvin.com

The Vineking
www.thevineking.co.uk
01737 248833

Vinology
www.vinology.co.uk
01789 264586

Vintage Roots
www.vintageroots.co.uk

Vinum
www.vinum.co.uk
020 8891 6010

Virgin Wines
www.virginwines.com
0870 164 9593

Wadebridge Wines
www.wadebridgewines.co.uk
01208 812692

Waitrose
www.waitrose.com
0800 188 884

Wheeler Cellars
www.wheelercellars.co.uk
01206 713560

Whitebridge Wines Ltd
www.whitebridgewines.co.uk
01785 817229

White Vin Man
01580 712826

Whole Foods Market
www.wholefoodsmarket.com

Wimbledon Wine Cellar
www.wimbledonwinecellar.com
020 8540 9979

Winedirect
www.winedirect.co.uk
0845 603 3717

Wine in Cornwall
www.wineincornwall.co.uk
01326 379426

Wineman.co.uk
www.wineman.co.uk

The Wine Press
www.winepress.biz
01228 515646

The Wine Society
www.thewinesociety.com
01438 740222

Wine Studio
www.wine-studio.co.uk
0845 085 8855

WoodWinters Wines & Whiskies
www.woodwinters.com
01786 834894

The World of Wines
www.worldofwine.co.uk
0845 430 9266

The Wright Wine and
  Whisky Company
www.wineandwhisky.co.uk
01756 700886

Yapp Brothers
www.yapp.co.uk
01747 860423

Stockists (Ireland)

Allied Drinks
www.cbrands.eu.com
+353 1 642 9500

Berry Bros & Rudd (Ireland)
www.bbr.com/ie.lml
+353 1 677 3444

Blakes Fine Wines
www.blakesfinewines.com
028 6774 8550

Booze.ie
www.booze.ie
+353 1 289 1288

Cabot & Co Fine Wines
www.cabotandco.com
+353 983 7000

Cassidy Wines
www.cassidywines.com
+353 1 295 4157

Celtic Whiskey Shop
www.celticwhiskeyshop.com
+353 1 675 9744

Comans
www.comans.ie
+353 1 451 9146

David Dennison Fine Wines
www.dennisonwines.com
051 853 777

Direct Wine Shipments
www.directwineshipments.com
028 905 08000

Egan's Wines
www.eganwines.com
+353 65 708 1430

Fallon & Byrne
www.fallonandbyrne.com
+353 1 472 1010

Febvre
www.febvre.ie
+353 1 216 1400

Findlater Grants Wine and
  Spirit Merchants
www.grantsofireland.ie
+353 1 630 4106

Galvins Wines and Spirits
www.galvinswines.com
+353 21 497 2200

Greenacres Wine Hall
www.greenacres.ie
+353 53 912 2975

Harry's Road Fine Wines
www.harrysroadfinewines.co.uk
028 92682818

James Nicholson
  Wine Merchant
www.jnwine.com
028 448 30091

Le Caveau
www.lecaveau.ie
+353 56 775 2166

Leinster Merchant Wines
www.merchantwines.com
+353 87 298 9387

Listons
+353 1 405 4779

Mark Jefferson Wines
07765 252322

McCabes Wines
www.mccabeswines.ie
+353 1 288 2037

Mill Wine Cellar
www.millwinecellar.ie
+353 1 6291022

Mitchell & Son Wine Merchant
www.mitchellandson.com
+353 1 2302301

O'Briens
www.obrienswine.ie
+353 1 850 269 777

Oddbins (Ireland)
www.oddbins.com
+353 1 667 3033

O'Donovans Off Licence
www.odonovansofflicence.com
021 429 6060

Power & Smullen Wine
  Merchant Ltd
www.pswine.ie
+353 1 610 0362

Russell's Cellars, Philip
  Russell Ltd
www.russellscellars.com
028 9 079 1919

Superquinn
www.superquinn.ie
+353 1 809 8500

Sweeneys Off Licence
+353 1 830 9593

Tindal Wine Merchants
www.tindalwine.com
+353 9673892

Uncorked
www.uncorked.ie
+03 53 1 495 0000

The Vintry
www.vintry.ie
+353 4905477

Wineonline.ie
www.wineonline.ie
+353 1 886 7732

Wines Direct
www.winesdirect.ie
+353 1 890 579 579

Wine Shop
028 6632 6948

Cheers

For Carls & Indi xx

Another year and another raft of people to thank for helping bring this edition of *The Juice* to life – here goes…

First up to Chris Terry, Matt Utber, and their respective teams: Jade, Lisa, and all the crew at The Plant, and Danny Tracy at Chris Terry Photography – massive thanks and respect for tireless efforts, good ideas and help, but mostly just for putting up with Chris. To my team: Debbie Catchpole and Verity O'Brien at Fresh Partners and Lisa Sullivan at One Management. To all the gang at Mitchell Beazley: Alison Goff, David Lamb, Hilary Lumsden, Becca Spry, Leanne Bryan, Fiona Smith, Tim Foster, Yasia Williams-Leedham and, in the same breath, Louise Sherwin-Stark and Kate Taperell at Hachette Australia. Huge love and thanks to you all. To my extended family: Fifteen Group (London, Cornwall, Amsterdam, and Melbourne), Jonathan Downey and Match Group (London, Ibiza, New York, Charmonix, and Melbourne), Frank van Haandel and Roger Fowler, Trevor Eastment at XYZ Networks, William Sitwell at *Waitrose Food Illustrated*, and Nick Scott at *GQ Australia*. And last but not least, to those behind the scenes including my amazing Mum (x), my brother Drew, Caroline, Jessie, Eve, Anne, Thommo, Gin, Camilla and Felix, Tobe, George, Randy, Pip, Gyros, BP, CC, and GG, Jamie and Jools, Danny McCubbin, David Gleave, Philip Rich, Stuart Gregor, Cam Mackenzie, Andy Frost, The Jones, Cooper-Terry, and Utber clans, Scania at Howies, Kate at Adidas Originals, Lucas and Indigo at Odo for keeping me awake with some of the best coffee south of the river, Dan Holland at Victoria Bitter, The Mighty Hawks, and beautiful Melbourne town.

M x